HIDDEN
HIGHWAYS
OF
CHESHIRE

Ten circular walks exploring Roman roads,
salters' ways, lost lanes, medieval roads,
and a complete Roman road.

TEXT AND MAPS BY

R J A DUTTON
© 1999

PUBLISHED BY

GORDON EMERY
27 Gladstone Road, Chester CH1 4BZ
01244 377955

PRINTED BY

MASONS DESIGN & PRINT, CHESTER.
Tel: 01244 674433

CREDITS

Thanks to Mr T Gleave of Peel Hall, Kingsley; Mr R Bate of Eden View, Bradley and Mr J Shore of Square House Farm, Dunham Hill for their help with additional information along the routes. Also thanks to Peter Jones of Pantymwyn, Oliver Park of Penyffordd, and Thomas Loughlin of Graianrhyd for their help on the walks. Moira Rae Carter linocut the cover design.

I am very grateful to the help given to me by Cheshire County Sites and Monuments Records Office for their help of interesting archaeological sites close to the walks.

As well as publishing, Gordon Emery walked all the routes with Ken Farrell, and helped with the text.

PUBLIC FOOTPATHS

All paths used in these routes are legal rights-of-way unless stated otherwise. Any problems such as missing signposts and obstructions have been reported to the appropriate Highways Authority.

Footpaths are the responsibility of the landowner or Highways Authority however the publisher would be happy to forward any letters to the right address with a copy to the Ramblers' Association who try to ensure that the councils carry out their legal duties to keep paths clear.

MAPS

No further maps are needed for these walks but it is advised that you carry an OS Pathfinder if you intend to leave the routes, or if you want to see where some of the Roman roads are going, beyond the walk given.

PUBLIC TRANSPORT

Wherever possible, the walks start from bus routes. Parking details are also given. Walkers should consult up-to-date timetables for leaving and return times before setting out.

CONTENTS

FOREWORD

The author first became interested in Roman roads during the early 1970s having once owned a field with a Roman road across one end of it. With some knowledge of ancient landscapes and construction methods he attended courses on the Roman period and so began to specialise in the search for the most difficult sections of Roman roads.

In 1985 he found most of the course of the Roman road between Chester and Warrington. This took almost eight years: a difficult task as the majority of the old road was under the later old Chester road and turnpike. Since then he has found several Roman roads across Cheshire. Having moved to North Wales in the late 1980s he has added Roman roads, Roman camps, Saxon sites and moated sites to an ever-growing list.

Two years ago he was persuaded to put his discoveries into print with 'Hidden Highways of North Wales'. Now he returns to his native Cheshire with this second book.

He hopes you will enjoy these walks and the thrill of walking in the footsteps of our ancestors. If you find other hidden highways he would only be too pleased to know.

INTRODUCTION

In Cheshire the land consists of a series of plateaux, one to the north between Mouldsworth and the River Weaver, a central one between Mouldsworth and Beeston, and a southern one reaching out from Peckforton to Malpas. Over the years artefacts have been found of Palaeolithic man and his weapons and tools of chipped and flaked flint.

The Romans made their mark on the pre-Cheshire landscape by their construction of a fortress and road centre at Chester (Deva) which was of strategic importance, between Celtic tribes, with access to the sea. Roman finds in Cheshire are fairly scant. It was once thought that much of the county was covered by a great woodland and little clearance took place for their agricultural needs. It is only in recent years that aerial photographs taken in long dry periods have produced more evidence of the Roman roads and practice camps through the county.

When the Romans finally left Britain in 410AD, invaders came from the north, Picts from Ireland, and later the Angles and the Saxons. Celtic rule lasted almost until the seventh century, two hundred years longer than in southeast England. Scandinavian communities settled into the Wirral leaving names ending in 'by' (Raby means boundary and it is possible that the Scandinavians had their own country north of this.) The Celts left their own place names in what is now Wales with 'Tre', 'Pen', 'Llan', and 'Maes'.

In the seventh century the Saxons were settled into farming communities. Names ending in 'Ley' suggest woodland clearances. Many of the old Cheshire village names give the hint of an old road, for example, Spurstow: 'stow' often implied a holy place and 'spor' meant a 'track' implying the existence of a road.

Later, the Normans constructed roads between their castles and large country estates. Their construction was very poor in comparison to the Roman roads, more often than not these roads were nothing more than earth tracks. In 1555 a great Highway Act was introduced, it placed responsibility for road repairs with the parish, this remained in force for almost three centuries.

Land or horse owners had to provide for four days a year *'one cart and two able men'*. Other householders, cottagers and labourers had to put in four days labour or send *'one sufficient labourer in his stead'*. The number of days was increased to six days in 1563. Unpaid surveyors were also appointed to inspect highways and bridges and had the right to dig gravel, without paying for it, for road repairs.

Unfortunately this act failed and the crude methods of road construction were inadequate to cope with the increase in traffic using the roads in the seventeen century, when wheeled carts were replacing the horse, and people were beginning to travel in coaches. Some form of central organisation for construction and repair was needed.

Medieval road found on Chester Infirmary site in 1998

In 1675, John Ogilby, 'Cosmographer', to King Charles ll published a book of highway routes between the major cities with the first 1 inch to 1 mile scale. A few years earlier, in 1663, the first Turnpike Act had arrived and was followed by many others in the eighteenth century.

The toll-roads were controlled by Turnpike Trusts who charged a toll at gates or bars along the routes. The improvement of these roads created their own form of genius with new road engineers in the form of: John

Metcalf (1717-1810) a blind man who lay stone sets with chippings to fill in the cracks; John Macadam (1756-1836) who used only local stone covered by a graduating smaller stone (he never used tarmacadam as believed); and Thomas Telford (1857-1837) who constructed the London to Holyhead road.

Not all the roads were kept in good condition, and not everyone wanted to pay the tolls. Salters' overland routes avoided the tollgates, and 'pikes' were put on top of the gates to prevent horsemen jumping over. In North Wales the 'Rebecca' movement had men disguised as women trying to wreck the gates.

These factors helped to bring about the eventual dismantling of the turnpikes so that by the end of the 19th century most roads were repaired by the county councils and the age of the toll roads had virtually ended, while another transport revolution, the railways, were in full steam.

Roads from throughout the ages are difficult to spot in Cheshire mainly because of the extensive farming throughout the county. Prehistoric tracks can still be found as footpaths over the hills but in the lowlands many have been ploughed away and only public footpaths remain.

Roman roads can still be found, but only on ground which has been untouched by the plough or in the Saxon names like Stretton and Heol. Some of the most obvious are marked on the OS map for the area. In the lowlands most are ploughed out or disguised by ditches and hedges criss-crossing them, while some have been reused into the modern system.

Bewick Woodcut

ROMAN ROADS FROM CHESTER
(NOT TO SCALE)

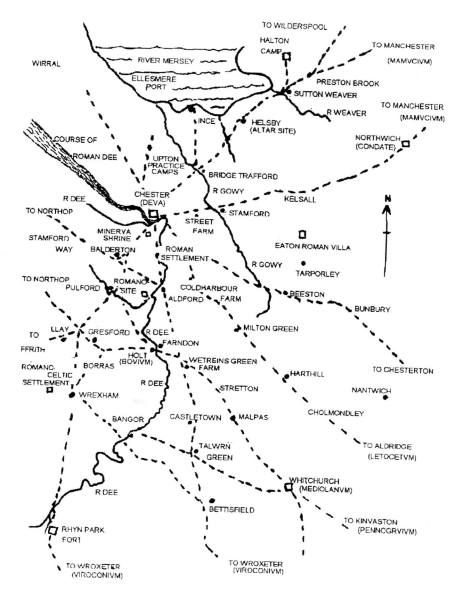

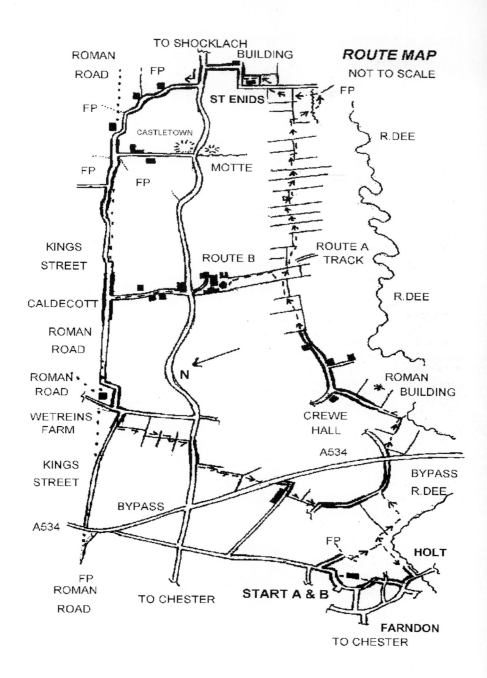

ROUTE MAP
NOT TO SCALE

TO SHOCKLACH
BUILDING
ROMAN ROAD
FP
ST ENIDS
FP
FP
R.DEE
CASTLETOWN
FP
MOTTE
FP
FP
KINGS STREET
ROUTE B
ROUTE A TRACK
R.DEE
CALDECOTT
ROMAN ROAD
ROMAN ROAD
N
ROMAN BUILDING
WETREINS FARM
CREWE HALL
KINGS STREET
A534
BYPASS
R.DEE
BYPASS
A534
FP
HOLT
FP
ROMAN ROAD
TO CHESTER
START A & B
FARNDON
TO CHESTER

Medieval Ways and a Roman Road
FARNDON

START
Farndon Church SJ 425546

Note: Some of the paths are liable to flood during the winter.
ROUTE A 8 Miles (13 Kms)
The walk goes alongside the River Dee and farm tracks, along a section of a long distantce footpath and several medieval roads, and a Roman road.

ROUTE B 5 Miles (8 Kms)
This is a shorter walk along the River Dee and farm tracks, along a medieval village road and a short section of a Roman road.

HOW TO GET THERE
By Car
Public Car Park in Church Street opposite the church.

By Bus
Bus Service between Chester and Malpas.

HISTORY
Results of excavation suggest that the church, St Chad's, stands within a Bronze Age settlement, a section of the defensive ditch system having been found on the southeast side of the churchyard. Part of the church was destroyed by fire and rebuilt in the 1600s. There are black and white houses in High Street and Church Lane. Some of the houses in High Street once had thatched roofs and one still has.

In the Domesday Book the village was known as Feredon (ferry town). It is likely that there was a ferry here from Roman times until a bridge was built. A ferry was recorded in 1315. The first stone bridge was built in 1338. It is recorded that the bridge is haunted by the ghosts of two Welsh princes who were thrown off the bridge to drown in the river, and their screams can still be heard on dark nights. In 1627 the bridge had 10 arches with a tower and a drawbridge on the fifth.Inside there was a small chapel dedicated to the Virgin Mary where travellers could pray before they completed their crossing.

On the 9th November 1643 Thomas Middleton (of Chirk Castle) leading the Parliamentary forces 'cast some grenados amongst the Welshmen' and captured the bridge but King Charles' army still held Holt Castle.

St Enid's Church at Castletown

DIRECTIONS

From the church follow the lane away from the village. Before the junction with the main road take the signed footpath, a wide track, on your right. When you reach the cross paths, turn right, and immediately left down the stepped path to the bank of the River Dee. Here, turn left along the boardwalk on the river bank. *If you look to your left you will notice the sandstone quarry that provided the stone for many of the houses in Farndon.*

Soon the boardwalk ends, continue along the river bank. At the 'Permissive Path to Meadows Lane' turn left, after looking back for views of Farndon Church, and Holt Church with its copper roof. In only 30 metres the path reaches the old lane (Meadows Lane). Cross the stile and turn right. Follow this under the Farndon bypass and as far as the left bend. Take the stile on your right, cross the field and climb the stile ahead. Follow the hedge on your right; when it comes to the bank of the Dee, turn left and carry on as far as the next fence. Cross and turn left; after the first field you will walk along a field access track.

Take note of the field on your right. During one dry summer the outline of a building was seen in the centre of this field from the air. A small excavation was carried out and it proved to be a Roman building. This field and the track that you are on are usually covered with flood waters from the river during a very wet season. With the finding of this building did this mean that the river did not flood in the Roman period ?

Proceed along the track and very soon it becomes used by farm vehicles as it climbs uphill towards the rear of Crewe Hall Farm. When you reach the council lane turn right, stop for a moment at a driveway by Crewe Place.

The drive goes to Crewe Hill House built upon high ground overlooking the River Dee. A few years ago the owner was extending the garden and found some roof tiles which were stamped Legio XX. These were made at the Roman tile factory near to Holt (Bovium). The logo which included the name and a wild boar, belonged to the twentieth legion that was based at Chester (Deva). Continue along the lane. After passing a cottage on your left with an old water pump, the lane becomes a grass track. Go through a fieldgate and follow the hedge on your right. When you reach the far side of the second field cross the stile which is twenty metres to your left. *If you look closely at the field surface immediately on your left you will see a darker line of grass running parallel to you, this was an old ditch that has been filled in.*

The shape of the surface that you are walking on gives another clue, for this was once part of the lane that you walked along from Crewe Hill. In the next field you can see where both ditches have been filled in. Unfortunately the road cannot be traced any further and it cannot be ascertained what date this road is from. However it is likely that it may have gone to either the old castle or the motte at Castletown.

ROUTE B Go to page 19.

ROUTE A
Turn half-right and cross the stile that can be found alongside the first field gate on your left. Proceed along the top of the bank and stop for a moment when you reach the trees. *Look back at the double hedge which runs down to the lower river meadows. This was an old road from Caldecote Village, it forded the River Dee and went to Is-y-coed.*

Cross the stile and plank bridge ahead. Carry on over two more stiles and plank bridges. Continue ahead to the far hedge and cross the double stile. Turn half-right and go over the next stile near the pond then turn left to the stile ahead. From here go half-right and continue for approximately two hundred metres and you will then see the next stile in the opposite hedge.

Continue straight ahead through the small gap to the right of the very wide gap in the hedge ahead. At the next corner of hedges, turn right over a plank bridge and stile. Turn left and keep to the hedge on your left and cross the stile in the lower part of the field. Proceed straight across the next field. Continue past the corner of the hedges on your right and walk on to cross the stile on your right.

The next stile is in the hedge on your left but to reach it by public footpath you should take a circuitous route by crossing the bridge over the stream and recrossing over another bridge again in 30 metres. When you reach the stile in the hedge stop for a moment. *Look across the river to a modernised farmhouse in the distance. This building is in England and yet the river, which in the majority of places is the border between England and Wales, is between you and the farmhouse. When the border was established along the course of the river in the eighteenth century, the river flowed on the far side*

13

of the farm. Since then, the river has moved to its present course leaving the border line on the far side of the farm. There are many places like this along the Dee.

THE WREXHAM ROAD
Climb the stile then walk half-right and go to the stile in the top right corner of the field which takes you onto a track and stop for a moment. *The track that you are now on was a medieval principal road. There was a large settlement on this side of the river, namely Castletown which was wiped out by the black death plague. The road went across the lower meadows and forded the River Dee, it then continued to Wrexham.*

The majority of the old road on the Wrexham side has been obliterated by the plough, but there are many references to it in early documents, particularly in the 'History of Farndon'. Cross the stile opposite and continue half-left across the small paddock to climb the stile in the top right corner. From here the path goes alongside the graveyard of St Enid's Church.

ST ENID'S CHURCH
Records can be traced as far back as 1575 but the church was probably much earlier. Originally it is likely that it was built for travellers to thank God for a safe crossing of the River Dee. The church once stood by a major medieval cross roads, one such road ran between Castletown motte and Shocklach. This road is only indicated by a public footpath today. For more information, leave the church grounds and turn right along the surfaced lane towards the small brick building. There is a write-up about the church and district on the notice board which is fastened on the east end of the small brick building.

CASTLETOWN
Ignore the footpaths and leave the church along the access lane that goes east to the Shocklach/Farndon road. At the junction, beware of the traffic, cross the road and turn left along the grass verge. When you reach the narrow lane on your right, stop for a moment. *Look directly ahead to a distant wood. In the wood and close to the present Farndon Road, are the remains of a Norman motte (an earth mound on which a wooden structure was constructed, this could have been either a tower or small rounded castle.) Opposite the motte, in a field to the right of the present road, there is another mound but of much wider and larger proportions, this was the remains of the stone castle mentioned in the notes at St Enid's Church.*

KING'S STREET

Turn right along the narrow lane to Castletown. *This part of the lane is only as old as the present Shocklach road.* Continue around the bends and by the second house on your right take note of the footpath pointer, I will mention this a little later. Carry on to where the lane bends to your left and stop for moment.

Look into the field ahead and you can see a ridge of high ground which runs from your left to right. This carries the remains of a Roman road and is also part of a parish boundary. Large sections of the road were reused by the Normans and re-named King's Street.

The Roman road ran south from Chester (Deva) to Wroxeter (Viroconium) near Shrewsbury. It went out of use when the modern system of roads were constructed. This section of the old road once contained a right-of-way but in later years it was closed. Remember the footpath I drew your attention to, the path is the re-route of the Roman road right-of-way.

After three fields the path rejoins the Roman road again and it continues to Shocklach. There is another right-of-way on the bend but this only goes to Tilston Village. Soon you will walk part of Kings Street which is in use as a byway and I will explain exactly where the original Roman road can be seen.

Continue along the lane and around the bends as far as where the modern metalling ends. Ignore the surfaced section of the road that goes into Castletown Farm. The road now becomes a byway. *You are now on King's Street.*

There is a footpath signposted on your left and this is the continuation of the Tilston path. Carry straight on and take note of the footpath pointer on your right, I shall refer to this later. Go around the right bend and where the track bends left there is a narrow track coming in from your right, stop here for a moment. *Originally this was the southwest entrance to Grafton Hall (near Tilston).*

Old entrance drives like these give a clue to the whereabouts of old major roads. The last footpath pointer is a re-route of the old right-of-way removed from the drive. Opposite the entrance drive look over the left hedge of King's Street; the Roman road originally was on that side. The most probable reason the Norman road was moved is the lack of maintenance of the Roman road. When it became very wet and boggy, travellers would have avoided this stretch, creating another road. When the Enclosure Acts came into force, the unused part of the Roman road would have been enclosed within a field.

King's Street

Carry on along King's Street, it suddenly becomes very wide. ***King's Street has now rejoined the Roman section***. Continue on; it is quite a long straight walk. ***In some parts the Roman road appears narrower but this is because an inner hedge has grown on your right.*** Soon the Caldecote village old road joins from your left. ***Here is another clue that you are on a major road.***

ROUTE B Joins here

The Caldecote road was a medieval road even though it may have been earlier. This is the track that I mentioned previously which went to Is-y-coed. The length between the small village and here has been widened at a later date. Proceed straight on along King's Street until you reach a point where you need to turn sharply to your left and stop for a moment.

TWO ROMAN ROADS

From here the Roman road continued ahead through Wetreins Green Farm. Here, there was a cross roads of the Holt (Bovium)/Whitchurch (Mediolanum) and Chester (Deva)/ Wroxeter (Viroconium) Roman roads. The Roman system by the farm has been enclosed and you may ask why this has happened.

It was most likely that these streets were still in use during the Dark Ages and the Norman period. Usually at a busy cross roads, a smithy or a small farm was set up, selling wares to travellers.

Over the years, the buildings expanded and therefore travellers would need to pass between the buildings. (There are many places still like this in Wales today). In the early fifteenth century large iron-wheeled transport vehicles began to appear and the principal roads that went through farms were too narrow for these vehicles to negotiate. New tracks were constructed around the buildings. Later under the Enclosure Acts field boundaries were erected or grown between the roads and fields.

MODERN ROADS

When the coach era arrived in the eighteenth century new roads were rapidly constructed throughout the county. In particular the Wrexham/Farndon to Nantwich turnpike brought about the present road system in the Shocklach and Tilston area.

Many of the existing tracks were closed down to wheeled vehicles and only contained the right-of-way for horses or walkers. Many of the large estates in those days still had the power to re-route or change the right-of-way to whatever suited their needs. Therefore King's Street was closed, only to remain as a byway in sections, and Whitchurch Street, being so close to a modern road, only retained the right-of-way in sections for foot travellers.

Proceed along the re-route until you reach the modern road by the farm buildings. Cross the road and turn left, then turn right into the byway which continues King's Street. *As you have probably guessed, this section that you are now on is not the original street.* Carry on for 400 metres as far as the footpath on your left and stop for a moment.

There is a very slight left bend in the track here. The length of King's Street ahead is the original Roman road. The latter length of the Whitchurch Roman route between the Wetriens and Holt is missing. This was most likely ploughed out; there is no evidence of its true route even on the 1947 aerial photographs.

TO FARNDON

Go over the plank bridge and across the field following the tree line. Cross the double stile ahead. Go through the gateway ahead and then through the gate on your right. Turn left, then go through the field gates to the road.

Turn right and walk along the road. Look on the left for the footpath sign. Cross the small stile and keep to the hedge on your left. When you reach a short crossing hedge and gap, bear right and keep the hedge on your left.

Cross the stile which is tucked in the left corner. Keep straight on from here and the next stile leads onto the Farndon bypass. Beware of the traffic and cross to the opposite side; go left to the railed path which you will see going up the bypass embankment. Proceed up this path and along the lane at the top. *This was the Crewe Hill Lane bisected by the new road.* When you reach the new bungalows on your right, go through the kissing gate which can be found on your left.

Continue down the field and go through the lower kissing gate and turn left, follow the enclosed track downhill and you will soon arrive at the permissive path that you came along from the banks of the Dee and Farndon. Once you have passed along the boarded walkway, instead of returning to the path that you came down, continue straight on and when you reach the river bridge stop for a moment.

The stone bridge was built in the fourteenth century. The remains of an earlier ferry point can be found on the Holt side of the river alongside the south side of the bridge and where a ford had once been. Further downstream away from the bridge and above the flood plain on the Holt side was the Roman tile factory. There may have been a small harbour somewhere close to the tile factory for shipping the tiles to Chester (Deva). To see the position of the former drawbridge go across the bridge into the field downstream and look back to see the rebuilt archway.

Turn right and proceed uphill along the pavement through Farndon village: when you reach the next lane on your right, turn right and walk up a steeper section to the church at the top. *The lane is earlier than the present main road and is assumed to be a medieval road that connected Farndon to Nantwich. Churches and chapels were often built alongside busy highways for rest and thanksgiving for a safe journey.*

ST CHAD'S CHURCH

There has been a building on this site ever since the Celtic period. Excavations by a team of archaeologists found that there had been a ditch and earth bank encircling the area. Most early villages where enclosed by some form of defence system and this may have been the case here. The church has a long and dramatic history dating from the fourteenth century. There is a booklet published by Cheshire County Council with a more detailed report of the history of Farndon. This can be obtained from local newsagents.

THE END

ROUTE B

Go across the field to the far hedge. Turn left and walk alongside the hedge on your right. When you reach the stile on your right by the farm building ignore this and turn left, walk around the rear of a deep concrete lagoon and then turn right. Continue straight on and pass between the cattle shed and silage store.

Leaving the farm buildings carry on along the farm entrance drive as far as the Farndon/Shocklach road. Go straight across and along the council lane past Caldecott Farm on your right. Proceed past the cottages on your left. *Look-out for the old water pump on your right.*

When you have passed this and reached the entrance drive to "The Cottage" on your right, the surface lane ends, but continues as a public bridleway along a stoned track. When this meets a crossing green road turn left.

Now go to page 16.

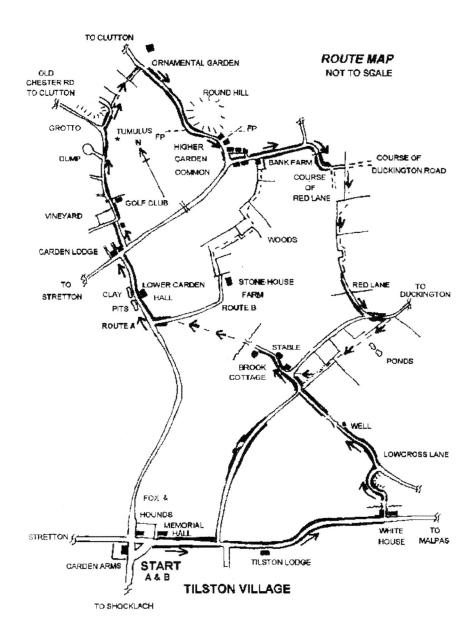

ROUTE MAP
NOT TO SCALE

TILSTON VILLAGE

20

Medieval Roads
TILSTON

START
The Fox and Hounds SJ 459513

ROUTE A 5 miles (8 Kms)
The walk takes you along a section of the medieval Chester road between Tilston and Carden Park, returning along other roads that were in use during that period.

ROUTE B 3 Miles (5 Kms)
The shorter route takes you along part of the medieval Chester road and through a wooded landscape, returning along other roads that were in use during that period.A small wood gets overgrown with nettles during the summer months, so take a walking stick.

There are places where the medieval roads go over private land. The walk then uses parallel public footpaths.

HOW TO GET THERE
By Car
Parking is available at the Fox and Hounds by request

By Bus
There is a bus service which runs from Chester to Tilston and Whitchurch
The bus stop is alongside the car park of the Fox & Hounds.

HISTORY
A village that dates from Saxon times, Tilston comprises four townships: Stretton, Carden, Horton and Grafton. The village once harboured smugglers, who followed a smugglers' walk across a ford by Stone House: one of the oldest houses in the village. The church dates back to the 14th century, it was the centre of village life, and the custom of rush bearing still continues; so do the annual wakes where the ox-roast takes place: the first slice sold to the highest bidder. Most of the cottages and houses stand on sites of older buildings. In recent years two new estates have been built.

21

Lowcross Lane was a medieval principal road that once ran to Chester. The lane branched from the Malpas to Aldford Roman road at Lowcross Hill. Travellers from Whitchurch could quite easily use the Roman road to Aldford, but by going this way they would need to ford the River Dee twice. This could be quite dangerous especially when the river was in flood. The Lowcross route avoided these fords and there was little difference in the mileage.

In the stocks

DIRECTIONS

Leave the Fox and Hounds car park and turn left along the pavement towards Malpas. When you reach the Tilston War Memorial Hall cross the road to the opposite pavement. Cross Inverish Road and continue ahead. *The Malpas road was laid over a Roman road that goes to Whitchurch. Little remains of the actual old road except for its reasonable straight course.* Soon you will walk downhill through a sandstone cutting. *This is from a later period, where steep sections of a road were lowered to aid horse transport.*

Continue past Tilston Lodge, set upon a high bank on your right, and follow the road downhill. When you see two white cottages on your left cross the road and turn left into a green lane before the first cottage. This is called Ford Lane, but the ford now has a footbridge. Follow this green lane around a wooded hill and you meet a surfaced lane. Stop for a moment. *You are about to join the medieval Chester road.*

22

Turn left along Lowcross Lane passing between the cottages. The lane goes uphill around a left bend and then descends to a sandstone bridge over a brook. Stop for a moment. *Take note of the hedge on your left. The way it runs down to the stream indicates that there was a shallow ford here. The ford was replaced by the bridge in 1935. Now look over the right parapet of the bridge. Below are the remains of an old well. This would have been at the same level as the older road.*

Proceed uphill around a left bend and soon the lane meets with the Hob Hill Lane. Turn right and go fifty metres, as far as the first cottage on your left. Here, turn left along a stone track. *You are still on the medieval road.* Carry on downhill past some stables on your right.

When I came along this lane there was a young lady bouncing up and down on the other side of the hedge. At first I thought she may have been on a trampoline. When I asked, she told me she was bouncing on a muck heap. Strange things that the country folk do!

Lower down, walk past Brook Cottage on your left and the stone track ends abruptly. The continuation of the trail is a narrow path directly ahead which goes down to a footbridge across the brook. Go through the small gate and climb the opposite side to the waymarked post. Stop for a moment.

If you crouch down and look at the sky line of the field to your left you may see a slight hollow in the field surface. This is the only remaining sign of the old road in the field.

Continue across the field (beware this path is sometimes illegally cropped and you will need to look for the waymarker on the other side of the field) and then climb the stile which leads onto a farm drive.

ROUTE B Turn right and go to page 28.

ROUTE A
Turn left and, at the modern road, turn right. **You are still on the medieval trail.**

As you walk along the road look along the left side and you will see man-made elongated ponds. These were originally medieval clay pits. The reason why they are shaped like this was a result of the clay being dug out by hand and loaded onto carts waiting on the roadside. Opposite the entrance of Lower Carden Hall you will see a sandstone bridge across these ponds.

This bridge is not very old and was constructed to hide the sewage pipe from the hall. When the road reaches a right bend the hollows disappears under the modern road. At the road junction ahead and by a lodge house go round the right bend.

The imposing sandstone gated lodge with its Greek Revival columns was the rear entrance to the former Carden Hall.

CARDEN HALL
In 1346 the local landowner was John who lived at Carden Hall. When his son became surgeon or 'leech' to Edward III, family fortunes increased. The hall was a beautiful timbered mansion and it was burned down in 1912, after which the family, now named Leech, moved to Stretton Hall. A branch of the family lived in Leche House, Watergate Street in Chester.

CARDEN PARK GOLF CLUB
Turn onto the stone track on your left signposted "Clutton". *This is the route of the medieval road.* Continue uphill until you reach the railed gates across the track. Go through the small gate on your left. Ignore the road on your left and carry on along the surfaced road. *Note the vineyard on your left. The golf club house on your right looks like a very large hotel.*

Beyond the club, the road becomes a stone track once more as it climbs further uphill, ignoring the three forks in the track to your left. *Along here the trees have been removed giving a fine view across west Cheshire and the Welsh hills in the far distance.*

STONE AGE
When you reach the fourth fork in the track stop for a moment. *When I reached this point there was a group of young trainee archaeologists from Liverpool University and Chester Archaeology lead by Keith Matthews.*

Small sections of ground just below the sandstone outcrop had been excavated and were being trowelled.

The site had been discovered by accident when pieces of flint were found thrown out of a rabbit burrow. By 1996 almost a hundred pieces had been gathered and excavations began that year. The trenches began to reveal evidence that people had used the cave in the late Mesolithic period (or Middle Stone Age, 6800-4300 BC). Beneath the Mesolithic finds they discovered a tool which may belong to the late Upper Palaeolithic (Old Stone Age, about 11,000-9000 BC), the period when people first returned to Britain after the Ice Age.There are also pieces of pottery that show that people were using the site in the Early Bronze Age (2300-1800 BC): scraps of human bone suggest that the cave was being used for burials at this time.

The story does not end in prehistory: a hermit lived in the cave between 1744 and about 1765. Along with the pieces of pieces of broken crockery and clay pipes that he may have used, it appears that he had a timber-framed front put onto the cave and the inside carved out to make life there more comfortable. Around the time the hermit left Carden, the owner of the estate, John Leche, built a pleasure garden there. His landscape architect transformed the cliff, carving niches into it, building a large earth platform overlooking the hall where he lived. He also designed the layout of the park.

Archaeologists at work

25

Go along the left fork for five metres and stop for a moment. *Look up to the sandstone overhang. There you will see the purpose-shaped large cave in the sandstone face; either side of the cave the sandstone is blackened. Beneath this there are iron stumps of lead plugged into the bedrock. Also slightly higher and driven deep into the sandstone face are iron bands. The irons either side of the recess were braziers, hence the blackened sandstone. This was the remains of the pleasure Grotto (picnic place with a view).*

The left fork, being the old Chester road, is likely to have been part of a Stone Age track. The Chester road continued downhill and through Clutton Village, crossing the fields to Aldersey Green and onward to Milton Green, where it joined a Roman road to Chester. (See the Milton Green walk.)

Leave the route of the Chester road and go back to the fork. Turn left, keeping the wooded hill on your left. *The trail that you are now on was the medieval Tattenhall road that branched from the Chester road.* Where the track bends sharp left, carry straight on across the course towards a cream and black house. Take the path between two fences then cross the stile onto the modern Tilston/Clutton lane and stop for a moment.

GARDEN ORNAMENTS
Walk across the road to the wood fence opposite and look across towards the black and white house. The largest part of the house is relatively modern but a small part dates to the sixteenth century. The sandstone walling in the garden and the dated archway, including the Ha Ha (raised lawn with ditch) were all constructed in the early part of 1998.

THE RETURN
It is time to make our return journey. Turn right and walk along the road. *This was a medieval road to Duckington and we shall follow it for quite a distance. In that period there would have been more trees along the way. Carden Park Golf Club are re-creating this with the tree plantation that lies along the right side of this road. Note the mature Field Maple; others have recently been planted.* Ignore any footpaths on the right or the left side. When the road bends sharply right you will arrive at Higher Carden Common bordered by cottages on your left. Turn left along a narrow lane which is signposted as a cul-de-sac. *This was the way of the Duckington road.* Continue downhill past Bank Farm on your right.

ROUTE B JOINS HERE

Take note of the walls either side of the lane, these were probably built by Carden Estate to keep the lane in a workable condition because the ground either side is higher and otherwise would have fallen inwards. Soon the lane levels and widens out. *The hedge along here dates to seven or eight hundred years old, therefore the lane was in use in the thirteenth century.*

To date a hedge count the number of established species, trees and shrubs, but not climbers, growing within thirty metres. Each species represents one hundred years. After you have found the total, add 10 years. This gives a reasonable date for the hedge. This hedge is about sixty metres long and it is the longest medieval hedge that I have seen in Cheshire, Usually these old hedges were not very long because medieval fields were only small. When you reach the sharp bend to your left. Follow the track which bends to the right and go through the gate.

RED LANE

Continue along the green road which goes around a left bend. Stop for a moment at the first field gate on your right.

This gate marks an old junction. The other road is known as Red Lane which went to Tilston. Originally it went across these fields but the18th century Enclosure Act closed it off. The public right-of-way has been moved. Soon you will be walking along it.

Continue around the bend and follow the track as it goes down into a hollow and reaches a fieldgate. Climb the stile. Stop for a moment. ***From here we leave the Duckington road that can be seen continuing across the fields ahead.*** Turn right. Keep the hedge on your right and cross the next stile and footbridge. Go half-right and cross the field to the footpath which goes alongside the hedge on your right.

At the far side of the field cross another stile. Keep alongside the hedge on your right again. Go around a pond, walk one hundred metres and climb the stile on your right. Turn left along the overgrown track. ***This is the continuation of Red Lane. When I was here in 1963 this track extended further along the fields.*** The growth along the lane soon falls away and from here walking is much easier to the modern Tilston/Duckington lane.

Red Lane

Turn left and in thirty metres go through the right of two gates on your right (signposted). Turn right and cross the field towards a protruding hedge corner. *When you are level with the ponds look to your right and you will see a short section of the medieval road between hedges.* Continue beside the protruding hedges. At the far end cross the stile. *You arrive onto another short section of the old road.*

Continue for fifty metres along the old road towards the farm ahead, then turn half-right and cross the field to climb the stile which takes you onto the modern road. Turn left, ignore Lowcross Lane from whence you came and continue on Hob Hill Lane around the right bend and straight on until it meets with the Malpas/Farndon road. Turn right and you are soon back at the car park.

THE END

ROUTE B
Proceed along the drive as far as Stone House Farm. Go through the field gate which has a notice attached "No Through Road" (This refers to vehicles and not walkers.) Proceed along the field access and when you reach the lower end

continue straight ahead keeping alongside the hedge on your left. When you have gone approximately two thirds of the way across the field, turn right and walk towards a short hedge which starts halfway across this part of the field.

Note this short hedge is made up of Damson and Cherry trees. These probably came from the days when farm workers carried fruit in their lunch boxes, and would spit the seeds or stones into the hedgerows. Keep the hedge on your right as far as the next crossing hedge. Here turn right and then immediately turn left to cross a stile and wooden footbridge in the corner of the field.

You are now entering a wooded area. The path bends to your left and then continues through a disused pheasant pen. *This area was a site of a farm. Although there is no visual evidence of it now, it is marked on earlier maps.*

Carry on past a small wire gate and the path bends to your right. Climb the stile on the edge of the woodland and proceed straight ahead keeping alongside the hedge on your left. Aim for the farm and climb the stiles ahead. Continue between the farm buildings and past a timber-framed brick infilled barn of the seventeenth century on your left. When you reach the farm gate onto the lane, turn right and go to page 27.

Bewick Woodcut

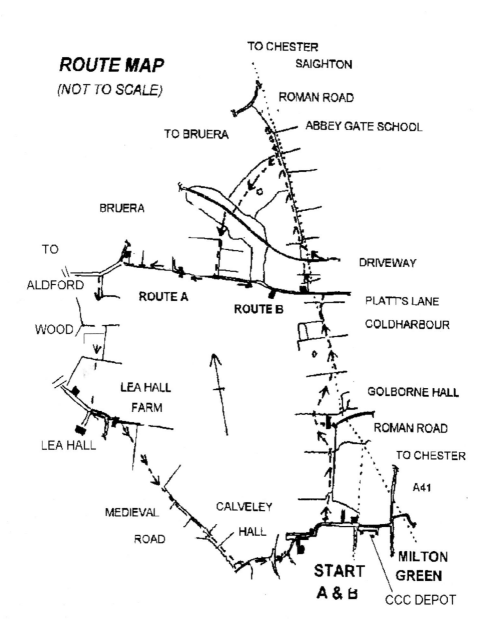

30

Roman and Medieval Roads
MILTON GREEN

START
Chapel Lane Milton Green (signposted CCC Depot) SJ 460587

ROUTE A   6 Miles (10 Kms)
The longer walk takes you along part of the route of a Roman road which ran between Chester and Wrenbury, returning along church paths and farmworkers' tracks, through a wooded avenue and along a medieval road crossing between two large estates.

ROUTE B   4 Miles (7Kms)
The short walk takes you along part of the Roman road and returns through a wooded avenue and past an ancient farm.

There are places where the Roman road goes over private land. This walk uses parallel footpaths but the route of the Roman road will be pointed out wherever possible.

HOW TO GET THERE
By Car
Parking area in Chapel Lane, Milton Green (signposted CCC Depot) SJ 460587

By Bus
Bus Service to Milton Green from Chester and Whitchurch

DIRECTIONS
Walk away from the main road along Chapel Lane. When you see a signposted footpath on your left, just past the council depot, stop for a moment. *If you look along the path which runs by the trees, it looks very like a road. Actually it was a main medieval road (see "The Tilston Walk"). This road originally branched from the Aldford/ Whitchurch Roman road by Lowcross Hill (Tilston) and joined another Roman road which ran between Chester and Wrenbury. In the early medieval period, travellers from Whitchurch to Chester needed to ford the River Dee twice if they used the Aldford Roman road.*

When the Dee was in full flood any wooden bridges at Aldford or Handbridge were quickly washed away. A new route was established connecting the Whitchurch road to the Wrenbury road. When the Chester Turnpike (A41) was constructed, the medieval road and the Roman Chester to Wrenbury roads were closed down. Only a public right-of-way existed. The problem in those days was that the large estates had the power to move the public right-of-ways to suit their field systems and this is what happened here.

If you look towards the house opposite, there is no right-of-way, although in the fields to the rear of the house the road was found running to a Roman ford on the Golborne Brook. The right-of-way between the house and the brook has been re-routed. The present lane ahead was an old drive connecting Caveley Hall to the medieval main route. Later the drive was extended to the turnpike.

Continue straight on along Chapel Lane, ignoring the track on your right, until you see a footpath signposted on your right before the bend. Cross the stile and go straight across the field. ***This is the re-routed right-of-way***.

Enter a small field access and enter the field on your left. (There was no stile at the time of writing.) From here turn right, follow the hedge and keep the wood and pond on your right to where there is a farmer's bridge over the Golborne Brook. Stop on this bridge for a moment.

Look over the right side. Below you will see the remains of a medieval sandstone bridge. In 1989 when I last walked this way the old bridge was in use but was slowly being worn away by the continual use of heavy farm vehicles. Beneath the bridge there was something much older: a paved ford indicating that there had been a way across this brook for many years. Probably this was an old track which ran between Golborne Hall and Calveley Hall.

ROMAN ROAD

Leave the bridge and walk around the farm ahead keeping the buildings on your right. There should be a footbridge here, if not in place, use the nearby farm bridge. Continue towards a fieldgate in the far hedge. When you reach the gate stop for a moment.

You are now on the course of the Chester/Wrenbury Roman road. There was evidence of the road across here in 1988, but since then there have been huge grants awarded by the Government to landowners to plough and grow, hence the road has been obliterated. Even the right-of-way has been re-routed in places. If you look back to Golborne Hall, the old hall is to the left of the farm buildings you have just passed. The Roman road ran between the hall and the field hedge to your left.

The road forded the Golborne Brook between the A41 and the hall. From there the road went southeast and by 1988 had disappeared towards properties at Milton Green. Further on, a long section of the road was found in use to the rear of Clayley Hall Farm (Tattenhall Lane). This section was re-used as a field access and was traced just beyond "The Righi" (house on the Tattenhall to Cowley Lane). Beyond the Cowley Lane the road disappears into the Bolsworth Estate. The road can be found again at Harthill reused in parts of the present Moss Lane (see the Bickerton Walk).

In September 1998 a section of the road was found in an estate southwest of Audlem. The road continued through Norton Hales and Loggerheads (Staffs). By using footpaths, bridleways and small lanes, the road was traced to Great Bridgeford (Staffs) where it joined a major route that ran between Stoke-on-Trent and Aldridge (Letocetvm).

Proceed through the gate and carry on straight across the field to the broken horse jump in the far hedge. Continue straight until you come to a protruding corner where two hedges meet. Carry on along the hedge on your left and go through the next gate on your left. Turn right and proceed alongside the hedge on your right. Carry on until you go through a fieldgate onto Platt's Lane. Turn left and continue along the lane to the stile on your right signposted 'Saighton'. Stop here for a moment.

Look further along the lane (west) to the farm entrance on the left. The name of this farm is on a wall: it is called "Coldharbour" Farm. On the First Edition 1873 OS Map it was called "Cold Arbour." There are several versions in England of Cold Arbour. Caldecote was another one, names all initiating from the Saxon period. Where there are names like these that are close to a Roman road, the remains of small buildings have been found close-by, often thought to be those of a stop-over for travellers.

33

No remains have ever come to light at Coldharbour Farm but it is likely that these may have been destroyed by the present farm buildings. Cross the stile on your right and go past the house on your left, continue over the next three stiles. Turn right along the Waverton Approach (Eaton Hall Drive). In a few metres take the stile on your left. Cross the stile and footbridge by the trees. Walk along the path which is alongside the hedge on your right. *The Roman road is on the opposite side of the hedge although there is no real evidence to see here. You will get a better view of it further on. To your left stands the Eaton Hall tower.*

SAIGHTON WAY

When you have crossed a stile and then a footbridge, stop for a moment when you reach the fieldgate on your right. *Look over the gate and here you will see a ten metre wide Roman road, intact, except for the paving slabs which would have formed the surface.*

Remains of Saighton Way

Walk further along the path and stop by the hedge which overlooks Abbey Gate School grounds. *Immediately below the hedge you can still see the Roman road but here there has been a pool dug deep through its old surface. Further along it enters a cutting (a lowering of the gradient).*

34

It has been re-instated as a garden feature, not by the occupants of the school, but by earlier owners. The Roman road continued its journey to Chester from the school and along part of the present Sandy Lane, the remainder being destroyed by the army camp at Huntington.

ABBEY GATE SCHOOL

Formerly known as Saighton Grange, years ago this was the main country house of the Abbot of Chester. Steeped in history, little remains of the original building. At one time the grange was probably the most outstanding house in Saighton.

CHURCH PATHS

Now the return journey is along footpaths used by people going to Bruera Church. Return the way you came. When you have crossed the footbridge, turn half-right. Cross the field keeping a large pond on your left. At the edge of the woods there is a small locked gate on a bridge. Climb the stile on the left side of the gate. Carry on through the woods. *When I entered these woods there was a fox about six yards ahead who seemed to be leading me along the path.*

The path breaks out onto the Waverton Approach. Turn right, then in three metres turn left onto the path (lots of undergrowth in the summer) through the remainder of the woods. *The fox was still leading the way.* At the edge of the woodland cross the stile into the field. *Here the fox got onto a step of the stile, stopped, looked back and seemed to be startled at the sight of me approaching. With one almighty leap the fox bounded over the stile and fled.*

Bewick Woodcut

35

Continue straight across the field keeping the large oaks on your right. Go along a field access and climb the next stile, then carry on along the path which runs alongside the hedge on your left. Get over the last stile onto Platt's Lane.

ROUTE B go to page 38.

ROUTE A
Turn right and walk along the lane as far as the first sharp right bend by the houses. Cross the stile directly ahead. *This is the way of the earlier Platt's Lane.*

BRUERA
Proceed on the path alongside the hedge on your left. At the next crossing hedge go through the fieldgate and straight ahead to go through the kissing gate and along a house driveway to the modern road. Here, turn left along the road and continue around the right and left bend. By the next right bend, and on the corner by some large iron gates, cross the stile on your left (signposted) in the corner of the field.

Coach House with Bell Tower at Lea Hall Farm

A CHURCH PATH

From this stile go half-right and follow the hedge. Two thirds of the way across this field, from the hedge corner go ahead to a gap in the hedge. Go straight through the small band of trees into the next field. Keep the hedge on your left then continue straight across the next field towards the bell tower which stands above the old Coachman's house at Lea Hall Farm.

MEDIEVAL ESTATE ROAD

On reaching the lane turn left and walk as far as the sharp right bend. Go into the farmyard: the bridleway goes straight through. Pass between the lagoon and the cattle sheds and onto a concrete field access ahead.

To the right of you there was once a moated site, probably the original Lea Hall. The bridleway follows the course of the medieval road past it. At the start of the concrete access turn half-right along the bridleway (signposted) across a cultivated field. At the next hedge continue on the same line and cross the field to the protruding hedge corner. Here proceed straight on keeping a hedge on your left. *When the field is ploughed cobbles show the course of the old road.*

At the next crossing hedge go through a bridlegate into the field and keep to the bridleway alongside the hedge on your left. *Along here you will notice that there is an outline of a road taking shape.* Go through the next bridlegate. *Now the existence of the road is present between two hedges. Further along the hedge has been removed but the cambered surface of the road is still present as far as the next gate. The road was probably constructed when the halls were established. It ran between Eaton Hall and Calveley Hall, once part of the Eaton Estate.*

CALVELEY HALL

Go across the bridge. *In this field the road has been ploughed out.* The bridleway is alongside the brook on your right. When you reach the small copse ahead, go left around the edge of the wood and carry on along a stone road. After leaving the wood, on your right there is a bridleway sign pointing the way along the field side of the hedge on your right. (If the field is too wet you can walk along the stone road as both meet at the far end of the hedge.)

37

Here there is a crossing stone road. Continue straight ahead and go through the bridlegate in the wooded railed fence. Along here the medieval road is clear from the reduced surface growth and an occasional outbreak of stones as it winds its way, following the trees, past the rear of Calveley Hall. *Originally the old road went to the front of the hall.* Beyond the hall and at the end of a cattle building go through a fieldgate into an area of rusting farm implements.

Continue with the track around a right bend and when you reach the cottages, turn left along the surfaced lane. Shortly you will arrive at the place where you started the walk.

THE END

ROUTE B
Turn left and continue straight on along Platt's Lane and go past Coldharbour Farm on your right. When you see the footpath fieldgate on your right, return on the same route that you came.

Asking the Way   From Coaching Days and Coaching Ways

38

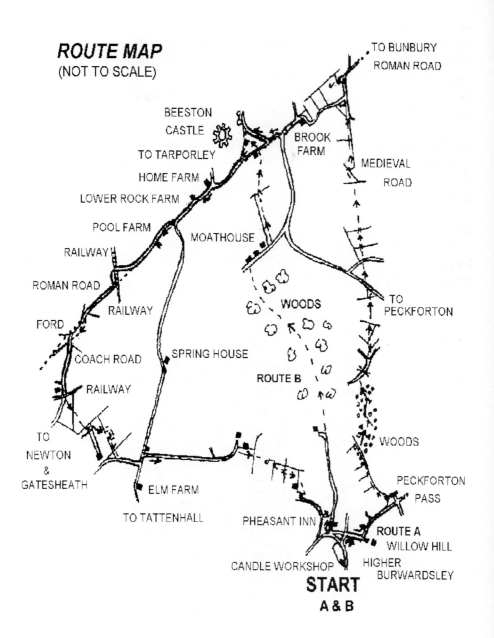

ROUTE MAP
(NOT TO SCALE)

TO BUNBURY
ROMAN ROAD

BEESTON
CASTLE

BROOK
FARM

MEDIEVAL
ROAD

TO TARPORLEY

HOME FARM

LOWER ROCK FARM

POOL FARM

MOATHOUSE

RAILWAY

ROMAN ROAD

RAILWAY

WOODS

TO
PECKFORTON

FORD

SPRING HOUSE

COACH ROAD

ROUTE B

RAILWAY

WOODS

TO
NEWTON
&
GATESHEATH

ELM FARM

PECKFORTON
PASS

TO TATTENHALL

PHEASANT INN

ROUTE A
WILLOW HILL

CANDLE WORKSHOP

HIGHER
BURWARDSLEY

START
A & B

39

Medieval Byeways, Roman and Coach Roads
BEESTON

START
Cheshire Workshops, Higher Burwardsley SJ 521564

ROUTE A 8 Miles (16 Km)
This is a walk along medieval roads, now only public rights-of-way, across the Cheshire landscape, also along a Roman road which has been replaced by a coach road in several places.

ROUTE B 6 Miles (10 Km)
The shorter walk takes you along an estate road through woodlands abundant with wildlife. The footpaths here have been re-routed away from medieval roads. Included is a walk along a Roman road re-used in parts by a coach road.

HOW TO GET THERE

By Car
Car park at the Cheshire Workshops.

By Bus
Bus service from Chester to Burwardsley.

DIRECTIONS

ROUTE B Go to page 52.

ROUTE B Go to page 52.

ROUTE A
Leave the car park and cross onto the lane ahead. At the cross roads turn right. When you reach the entrance to Willow Hill Farm go around the sharp left bend and stop for a moment. *Look back at the stile which is on a line with the part of the lane where you have stopped. In the twelfth century principal roads between large estates were merely rough stone tracks, some, more often than not, only three metres wide. There were no boundary hedges to contain travellers.*

The lane that you are on and the right-of-way beyond the stile was a principal route between Tattenhall Hall and Cholmondeley Castle Estate. (See the Bickerton Walk.) The lane goes uphill and through the Peckforton Gap on its way to the Cholomondeley Estate.

Carry on along the lane as far as the right bend and stop for a moment. *Look at the entrance drive on your left which now only goes to a cottage. This track was also once a principal road. It originally went to Bunbury. Very soon you will walk a section of it.*

In the late seventeenth century a new system of roads became necessary for farmers and land owners to transport their wares by wheeled vehicles to market towns. Large estate owners, not wanting any public transport passing through their grounds, paid to have the new roads laid around their boundaries.

The old principal routes went out of use because they were too narrow, deeply rutted and, more often than not, they only linked the estates. These old routes were closed off leaving only a public right-of-way for foot travellers. In many cases these rights-of-way have been moved to suit the ever- changing farming needs, but in many cases the original routes can be found either by searching through old estate documents or in actual field research.

PECKFORTON GAP
Go as far as the top of the gap by a sandstone lodge. *Look down into the pass, signposted 'Bulkeley Village'. It does not give the impression that a road once went this way. This is because over the years the pass has become very worn down by many walkers, but I can assure you there was a road, for it can be found to the rear of the houses at the lower end of the pass.*

Return twenty metres the way you came and take the stile on your right alongside a tall sandstone wall. This path is part of the Sandstone Trail: a long distance footpath that runs through Cheshire from Beacon Hill near Frodsham to Grindley Brook near Whitchurch. Follow the trail keeping the wall on your right, cross two stiles and, when you are walking through a narrow enclosed section, take the path beside an oak tree on your right and just before the third stile.

BUNBURY ROAD

You are now on the old Bunbury road. The road has been destroyed by the estate plantation, but if you keep your eyes on the path there are several places where the old road reveals itself. Follow the path through the woods. In only a few metres, when you see a wooden signpost ahead, turn left. The main trail soon sweeps right. *When you walk along this next section you will see parts of the old road which have been left intact.*

At both forest roads turn left. Exit onto an old road that is constructed of sandstone sets. *Here is another principal road that connects the village of Peckforton and Higher Burwardsley. This road is still in constant use as it is the shortest way between the two villages.*

Turn right and walk downhill, and under the archway of a stone bridge which supports an estate road overhead. *Note the large stones protecting the structure from damage by wheeled vehicles.* Continue downhill through a field gate across the old road, then turn sharp left up a stone track. Go ten metres and take the narrow path on your right which climbs up the bank above the old road. Proceed down the slope alongside a wire field fence on your left and cross the stile lower down. Stop here for a moment. *You will see a track which turns slightly left and disappears into the woods. This is the continuation of the Bunbury road. The public right-of-way has been moved to the lower fields.*

Turn half-right and take the next stile in a short distance; stop here for a moment. *Look to the edge of the wood further up the hill and you may see the old road skirting the edge of the woodland running parallel to the public footpath that you are on.* Turn half-right once again and go to the next stile. From here follow the worn trail over the large field. You need to cross two stiles set close together; the path then exits onto the Beeston road. Turn left along the road and in a short distance cross a stile on your right signposted 'Bunbury' and 'Beeston Moss'.

The old Bunbury road would have descended from the hills, but it has been obliterated in the lower fields. The stile that you climbed is on the line of the old road. Across the fields the footpath follows the actual route. There is no remaining evidence of the road until you get into the sixth field.

Go half-left and proceed across the field. Climb a stile to cross a farm track and another stile opposite into the next field. Carry on straight ahead to a footbridge across a small stream. Continue in the same direction to a stile ahead and another footbridge. *On your left, Peckforton Mere is hidden by trees but attracts Canadian Geese into these fields to feed.* Resume straight on across this field and climb a stile alongside a horse jump.

From here it is but a short walk to the next stile on your right, and an open vista of Peckforton and Beeston castles to your left. At the start of the woods, go half-right and cross this field towards the hedge on the far side. *Here you will find the remains of the old road.*

Continue keeping the hedge on your right side. *You are now on the Bunbury road, between the oak trees.*

When you have crossed two stiles you will see that the old road is now enclosed by a hedge either side. ***Beyond the stile is a crossing road which was a Roman road re-used in the Middle Ages. It branched from a major road near Beeston village and goes through Spurstow to Wrenbury (see the Bickerton Walk).*** *Try to imagine what it would have been like in the early medieval days, the fields being nothing more than wooded areas; making the roads very dark and dangerous places to travel.*

Proceed straight ahead along the enclosed road signposted 'Bunbury' which soon becomes an entrance lane to the cottages on your left. Carry on until the old track joins with the Beeston/Bunbury modern road. Beware of the traffic and turn right. Follow the modern road as far as the cottages on your left. Immediately past the semi-detached cottages cross the stile on your left signposted 'Beeston' and 'Beeston Brook'.

A PRINCIPLE ROMAN ROAD
You are now on what was the route of the Chester/Chesterton Roman road. Ploughing has completely obliterated any evidence but it could be seen on aerial photographs in 1948. The most likely reason why it was closed to public use was that the road may have become waterlogged and when the coach era came it was decided to construct a new road around the field to where the modern road is today.

Follow the hedge on your left and cross the next stile into a very large field. From here bear slightly left across this field. Ignoring the stile on your right, head for the gap between the castles. The footpath runs parallel to the Beeston road which is on the other side of the field hedge to your left.

From here you will see the stile ahead. Continue over another and ignore the stile on your left which leads onto the modern road. Keep straight on and climb the next stile from which you can see a stile ahead which leads onto the Beeston road. Beware of the traffic and turn right.

The farm on your left is Brook Farm and dates from the sixteenth century. **The farm was built beside the Roman road.** Proceed along the present road and, at the road junction of the Beeston/Peckforton road, turn left. When you reach the left bend by the old cottages turn right along Tattenhall Lane. ***This is the continuation of the Roman road and coach road.*** When you reach the houses on your left, turn right into a narrow lane. You soon reach the sharp right bend by Beeston Castle wall. *There is a car park on your left and a refreshment stall which is open most week-ends.*

BEESTON CASTLE
Although isolated, Beeston Crag is part of a chain of hills stretching across Cheshire from north to south. Beeston was long thought to be a possible settlement site, but only recent excavations have proved the matter beyond doubt. Remains have been found of a Bronze Age community living here about 800BC.

Excavations have also shown that about four hundred years later there was a fortified bank and ditch on the part most vulnerable to attack. Protected by these defences, an Iron Age settlement flourished here. Some of the finds are on exhibition at the castle entrance. The hill fort was abandoned, probably by the beginning of the Roman period. A few Roman finds have come from the base of the hill, as well the hint of a Roman road. The hill emerges from the shadows again in 1225 when the castle was built by Ranulf, the sixth Earl of Chester, following his return from the Crusades. The castle was seized by King Henry III in 1237 and it remained in royal ownership until the sixteenth century. It was refortified during the Civil War, when the Royalists' garrison was besieged by Parliamentary forces, and finally surrendered in 1645.

The castle is open to visitors between April and September. The gatehouse museum and craft shop are worth a visit. The majestic castle standing on a sheer outcrop of Cheshire rock has the most stunning views of the surrounding countryside of any other castle in England.

Turn left, and take the footpath between the castle wall and car park hedge. When you reach the woods there is a fork in the path.

ROUTE B joins here

Keep right, along the path that goes downhill beside the castle wall. Climb the stile which leads onto Tattenhall Lane. Stop for a moment. *You are now back on the Roman road. Part of the Roman system was re-used as a coach road and some sections are incorporated into the modern system. I will point out where the changes take place as you walk along the road.*

Turn right along the lane. *Note the sheer height of the castle rock on your right. During the Civil War, just before dawn on the 13th December 1643, a Captain Thomas Sandford with 8 other Royalists is believed to have scaled these precipitous cliffs to gain entry to the castle. He then persuaded the Parliamentary garrison of sixty men commanded by Captain Thomas Steele to surrender. It is not known exactly where they scaled the cliffs.*

Continue past the rock, ignoring the lane on your right, and walk past Home Farm. *Keep an eye on the hedge on your right. When you are approaching Lower Rock Farm, on the right, you will see that the hedge points towards the farm buildings. Nearer the farm the hedge has been stopped and a much younger hedge returns back towards the road. The older hedge indicates the older road went nearer to the farm. The section of the modern road that curves left and right around the farm was the coach road. When you have gone past the farm the road bends left again and you are back on the Roman system.*

Continue until you reach the very sharp left bend. *Here the modern system now goes to Tattenhall.* Turn right along the small lane. *This is the Roman and coach road.* The initial part of the lane is surfaced and it bends right and then left. *There was a good reason for these bends. There was once a very large deep and wide pool on the direct line of the Roman road.*

45

This is one occasion where the Romans would bend a road. The landowner has since filled this pool and only a small pool remains further along. As you walk along the lane take note of the original width of the Roman road, from ditch to ditch either side.

The chipped surface only goes as far as Pool Farm and then the road becomes a stone track. On the approach to a railway bridge there is a field gate on your left. Stop for moment. *This was where the Roman and coach road originally went through before the construction of the railway.* Go over the railway bridge and around the left bend and continue as far as the next right bend. Stop here for a moment. *This is where the old roads were cut by the railway; you are now back on the original route.*

Carry on along the track and you will notice that there is a layer of small sandstone blocks under foot. *These were the original surface of the coach road.*

Coach Road

During 1993 a colleague and I cleared a one metre wide strip across the road and cleaned off the sandstone blocks. This revealed a coach road of three metres wide. A trench was then cut through this surface to reveal the remains of the Roman road beneath. The Roman road was ten metres wide. A report of the excavation was deposited with the local Authority.

As you walk along this section you will notice that you are on a central ridge and the land falls away either side. Further on there is a gradual descent in the route and eventually the road narrows and in places becomes very wet. This is because the road is approaching a ford that has suffered much abuse from later traffic and no maintenance.

When you have reached the lowest level cross the stile which you will see on your left. Turn right and stop for a moment. *You will notice that there is no hedge along this side. In the 1920s the ford and surrounding ground was in a terrible state. The Parish Council with a group of local farmers infilled the land where the path now runs. A stream that once crossed here was changed to its present course. The section of the old road between the ford area and the stile that you have just climbed was closed to traffic.*

Continue twenty metres and cross the stile. Stop for a moment. *Look to your left and at the large bushes, These hide the continuation of the coach road. Now look back to the first stile. The ford was once halfway between the two stiles. The brook on your right is on the later course. If you look into the right bend of the brook you will see large stones which belonged to the coach road.*

Follow the brook a few paces to the hedge opposite you. **Look into the stream bed here and there are heaped rounded small stones. These stones are from the Roman road proving that the stream has cut through the road. If the Roman ford had been here, the stones would have been large and flat shaped.**

Turn left and go to the entrance of a narrow track on your right and stop here for a moment. **Look to the hedge that you just walked along. This hedge is not very old and to the rear the ground has also been infilled. It is all black soil to a depth level with the part of the road that you are now standing on.**

The entrance to the narrow track has been turned to meet the coach road. Further away from you the track gets much wider. This is the continuation of the Roman road, but further along still it has been destroyed by a canal. The Roman road did not suit the 17th century system so it was stopped off. The narrow track was deliberately constructed so that travellers with wide carts could not use it, thereby forcing all users along the coach system and, of course, through the toll-gates. The narrow track later became an entrance road to Huxley Mill.

Paying Toll *From Coaching Days and Coaching Ways*

The Roman road was traced west-northwest past Huxley Mill Farm and across the fields to the southwest of Higher Huxley Hall, becoming part of the modern Huxley Lane by Haven Cottage and leaving again before Golden Nook Farm. The old road went across the fields and became a section of Long Lane near Milners Heath. Before Waverton Church the Roman road leaves the modern system once again to continue across the fields outlined by the present footpaths and hedgerows. It crossed the A41 slightly north of Smithy Farm, near Rowton. The old road eventually disappears in the direction of Huntingdon. It is thought that it may have joined the Manchester Roman road at Boughton (Chester).

THE RETURN

It is time to make the return journey. Leave the ford area and proceed along the stone track ahead of you. *This track was constructed to enable carts to reach the infill site. If you look through the hedge on your left you see the remains of the coach road and its outer ditch.*

The stone from this road has been removed and probably used in the infill of the lower fields. Further along track and coach road combine. The width of the coach road varies between three metres and five metres, whereas the width of the Roman road was fairly constant.

You may wonder if this section of the coach road might be of Roman origin. I can assure you it is not: Roman roads are constructed reasonably straight. If you look at the course of the coach road there is a large dog-leg from the ford.

The coach road continues to where it has been incorporated into the modern Newton Lane. It then goes past the Cheshire Farm (Ice Cream Factory). At Gatesheath the old road runs along part of a Parish Boundary, slightly north of the present lane. It then combines with an old road from Tattenhall. The name Gatesheath refers to a toll-gate. The road then continued west to meet with the Chester/Whitchurch turnpike (A41.) There was no road continuing west from the junction.

Proceed along the coach road as far as the railway tunnel. When you have gone through the tunnel, immediately turn left and climb up the embankment. Cross the stile at the top. Go half-right across the field. You will only see the

49

next stile on your left when you approach a wooded pond. Cross this and go half-right towards a stile by a field gate ahead. Turn left along the farm field access as far as the sharp right bend, then go over the stile directly ahead.

SPRINGS

Turn half-right once again and cross the field towards two trees which are reasonably close together; go over the footbridge between the trees. Turn right, walk around the pond, and continue to the next footbridge in the corner of the field. There is another small pond on your right. Go twenty metres to a stile on your right which leads onto the Newton Lane. Turn left and proceed to where the lane meets the Tattenhall/Beeston road. Stop for a moment. *Look left along the Tattenhall Lane as far as the distant bend. Just beyond, there is a property which may be seen through the trees. This is Spring House; a thatched property dating to the sixteenth century. The building is in the centre of a system of fresh water springs.*

Spring House, Tattenhall Lane

In the medieval period fresh water was carted in barrels from there to Tattenhall. It was the only known source of fresh water in the area. Now look to your right to where the modern road bends left by Elm Farm. The original track did not bend but continued straight across the fields directly to Tattenhall Village. Clues to this can be found in old documents and also visually. The hedge on the present bend has been implanted with a different species. At Tattenhall there is a short section of the old track still in use.

Turn left and immediately turn right into Wood Lane. Walk along this lane ignoring any of the smaller lanes on the left and the right. At the end of the road proceed along a cobbled farm entrance drive. When you see a sandstone wall ahead, climb the stone stepping stones over the wall into a field. Walk straight ahead keeping the farm buildings and a barn dovecote on your left.

Ignore the stile on your left which is immediately at the end of the buildings. When you have reached this point you will see your next stile directly ahead. Cross the footbridge and continue directly uphill. At the top of the hilly field the path goes to the left side of a solitary oak tree which has a waymarker on its trunk; the path then descends past another tree by a large round cattle trough, and then goes downhill. The stile is on your right alongside a field gate. Stop here for a moment. *Look at the track which goes from this gate towards the farm on the opposite slope. Keep this in mind because I shall refer to it later.*

Proceed downhill to cross the footbridge. Continue up the other side of the valley to a stile in a fence. Turn right and follow the path which keeps the farmhouse on your right. Cross the stile onto the farm access drive and turn left uphill.

When you reach the band of trees on your right side, stop for a moment. *If you look carefully under the trees and lower than the lane, you will see the earlier farm road which looks like a wide dried-up brook.*

Carry on around a right bend and turn left into a narrow grass track which goes uphill. Stop for a moment. *Remember the cobbled farm entrance drive that you entered from Wood Lane and the track that I drew your attention to at the rear of the last farm.*

The old road in the trees which you have just seen and this track that you are on was one road which was one of the old principal routes that connected several farms between Huxley and Burwardsley.

Continue uphill and as far as a crossing surfaced lane. Turn right along the lane which takes you by the Pheasant Inn on your left. Continue straight across the crossroads and soon you are back at the Cheshire Workshops' car park.
THE END

51

ROUTE B

Leave the car park and turn left along the lane and continue straight on. When you reach the cross roads, proceed straight across and walk by the Pheasant Inn on your right. *Along this old lane on your right you will see several old cottages refurbished in keeping with their original style.*

When you reach the end of the lane, by the entrance to Spring House, go through the small gate ahead, and along a forest track. Follow the signposts for Beeston. When you have reached a signed cross paths continue straight on. You are now on part of the Sandstone Trail. Continue downhill and exit onto the road. Here turn right and continue past all the old converted properties along the left side of the road. Ignore the first footpath sign on your left but turn left at the second footpath which is signposted 'Beeston Castle'.

Carry on over the field keeping to the path alongside the hedge on your left. Lower down the field the path descends to a footbridge and goes up steps on the opposite side. Here the footpath is purpose-made, so do not stray. Eventually the path exits onto the Tattenhall Lane by Tabernacle Cottage. Beware of the traffic and cross the road.

Climb the stile opposite and proceed along the path through the woods. The path goes uphill and alongside a field fence on your right. When the path meets another path by the castle wall, turn left and go to page 45.

Bewick Woodcut

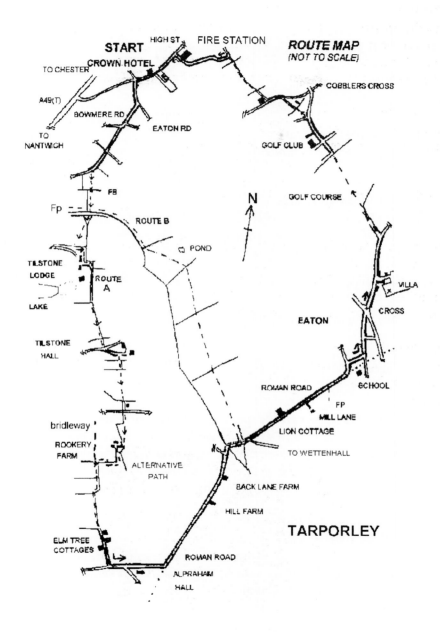

START
HIGH ST   FIRE STATION   **ROUTE MAP**
CROWN HOTEL   *(NOT TO SCALE)*
TO CHESTER
                                          COBBLERS CROSS
A49(T)
BOWMERE RD
                                          GOLF CLUB
TO   EATON RD
NANTWICH

                                          N

                FB   GOLF COURSE
Fp
        ROUTE B

                        POND

TILSTONE
LODGE   ROUTE
            A   VILLA
LAKE   CROSS

TILSTONE   EATON
HALL

                                  ROMAN ROAD   SCHOOL
                                          FP
                                          MILL LANE
bridleway   LION COTTAGE
ROOKERY
FARM   TO WETTENHALL
            ALTERNATIVE
            PATH
                                  BACK LANE FARM

                                  HILL FARM

ELM TREE   **TARPORLEY**
COTTAGES
                        ROMAN ROAD
                        ALPRAHAM
                        HALL

53

Medieval Roads, a Roman Road and a Roman Villa
TARPORLEY

START
Crown Hotel   SJ 555623

ROUTE A   6 Miles (10Kms)
A walk along a medieval estate road and a Roman road, passing Eaton Roman Villa, and returning by a medieval road.

ROUTE B   4 Miles (6 Kms)
A shorter walk along the medieval estate road and an estate workers' footpath, returning along a short section of a Roman road, passing Eaton Roman Villa, and finally a medieval road.

HOW TO GET THERE
By Car
Parking is available to the rear of the British Legion opposite the Crown Hotel.

By Bus
Bus service between Chester and Nantwich

HISTORY
The Swan Hotel, the Manor House and the 13th century church were the focal point of Tarporley village life. Old families, the Dones and Earls of Haddington, were generous benefactors to the village: the village hall, a listed building, is called the Done Room. The Tarporley Church records date from the 13th century, the church itself being restored in Victorian times.

EATON ROMAN VILLA
Unfortunately, at the time of writing, the landowners are not allowing general access to the interesting villa site. Contact Environmental Planning at Cheshire County Council, Commerce House, Hunter Street in Chester to find out present and future access arrangements.

DIRECTIONS

Walk from the Crown Hotel away from the village centre. Immediately past the Foresters Arms take the zebra crossing, then go down Eaton Road ahead. When you reach the road fork bear right along Bowmere Road, Walk past the houses and, where this road bends right, turn half-left along the narrow lane.

The part of Bowmere Road that you have just walked and this lane formed a medieval road. It originally came from Alpraham Green and connected Tilstone Hall and Tilstone Lodge with Tarporley.

TILSTONE LODGE

When you reach the cross roads beware of the traffic and go straight across. Continue around the right bend and look for the first field gate on your left. Proceed over the stile beside the gate and go straight across the field. When you are two thirds across the field walk towards a lone oak tree which stands away from the far hedge. From this tree go straight on for 15 metres to a footbridge over the stream. Across the next field go alongside the hedge on your right. At the far end of the field ignore the stile on your right. *You are still on the route of the medieval road.*

ROUTE B

Turn left, ignore the small gate on your right and go to page 63.

ROUTE A

Turn left and go through a small gate on your right leading into a wooded avenue. *This avenue formed a boundary around Tilstone Lodge and terminated at Tilstone Hall.*

Continue through the next gate and cross the stile on your right in 15 metres. From here go half-left and climb the stile alongside an electric pole. Turn left and go down the grass slope, then turn right by the fence. Go across the concrete yard by the old cattle sheds; at the end of the tall wooden railed fence turn left. Turn right immediately at the far end of the corrugated haybarn. Proceed along a field access track. *Note the gardens on your right which belong to Tilstone Lodge. If you look carefully at the grass area between you and the house there is a sunken hollow which goes towards the house. This was the northern end of the large lake which now lies between the house and the A51.*

TILSTONE HALL

Go through the gate at the end of the track and continue alongside the railed fence on your left. *This field is often inhabited by Canada Geese.* Cross the stile ahead and go through a gate onto the entrance drive of Tilstone Hall. *The original hall was demolished in 1736, the present one being built in 1820-30.*

Turn half-left, ignore the green access drive immediately on the left, and go along the used farm drive. When you reach the bend in the sandstone wall on your right, turn right through the concrete silage store. Proceed straight across the field towards a house at the far side. Two-thirds across the field go to your right of the house and pass through a gate onto a rough overgrown track.

This is the only visible section of the medieval road that displays how it originally looked. All other evidence has either been completely obliterated by the plough, changing field systems or the present road system.

ELM TREE COTTAGE LANE

Climb the stile at the end of this section of the old road and cross Brains Lane to climb the stile opposite, walk alongside the hedge on your right. When you reach the end of the hedge go half-right and proceed to the rear corner of Rookery Farm.

It is the Tithe map that gives a clue to the route of the medieval road across the Rookery fields. There are also indications of the right-of-way being changed several times to suit the ever-changing farming needs.

From the corner of the farm go half-right and cross the double stile and footbridge which lies close to the farm buildings on your right. The next section of the path is often overgrown.

The farmer has given permission for walkers to keep the hedge ahead on their right and cross back to the path using the next gate on your right, ensuring its closure, then turn left. Walk alongside the hedge on your left and go through the bridlegate on your left. *You are still on the medieval road.*

Follow the waymarkers alongside the hedge until you reach the last gate that leads onto Elm Tree Cottage Lane.

As you walk along the lane take note of the timber-framed cottages either side. These date from approximately the sixteenth century or possibly earlier. They are a good indication that a medieval road passed through here.

THE RETURN

It is time to make the return journey. When you reach the road junction ahead, turn left along the lane. Ignoring the lane on the right, continue past Alpraham Hall on your right. Stop for a moment on the sharp left bend. *You are now on a Roman road. It originally came across the fields from your right. The road is thought to have branched from a main street running between Tarporley and Nantwich.*

Continue along the lane. *Take note of its width ditch to ditch, much wider than lanes constructed in the medieval period. Further on I will draw your attention once again to the construction and you will see quite a difference.*

Carry on past Hill Farm (beware of the dogs here; they come out behind you but are usually only noisy and soon will return to the farm). Walk past Back Lane Farm on your right and ignore the lane on your left. When you go around the right bend and onto the straight ahead, stop once more.

ROUTE B joins here
If you had been walking the road in the Roman period you would have just crossed a ford, hence the turn. Look at the construction here, huge earth banks raise towards the crown. The central reservation has been raised due to the ground either side once being very wet. There is another left bend where, once again, there was another ford.

This road was traced from Calveley to Preston Brook (on the A56 near Warrington). The road goes north past the perimeter of Eaton village and is re-used by the B5152 to Hatchmere. There, the Roman road leaves the modern highway and can be traced across the fields by either footpaths and hedgerows that fall onto its line. On the outskirts of Kingsley the road was re-used as an access to Hall-o-th-Hay. Beyond the hall is the River Weaver. Before the river was widened there was a crossing called the Kingsley Ford. The road then continued along present tracks and lanes to Preston Brook, where it joined the Street, a Roman road between Chester (Deva) to Warrington (Wilderspool). See the last chapter THE STREET.

Ignore Wettenhall Lane but carry on along the Eyton and Tarporley lane. *Keep an eye out for a small building on your left, known as Lion Cottage. There are two small stone lions inset into the upper walls.*

Lion Cottage

If any reader knows the history of these cottages and the lions would you please let me know as neither I nor the owners can find anything recorded about them.

Proceed ahead, ignore the lane opposite Winterford Farm and carry straight on. **When the lane bends sharp left you are now leaving the route of the Roman road and entering Eaton Village.** Turn right into the first road on your right. *This is named Winterford Lane: a medieval road which replaced the Roman road that crossed the fields to the rear of the new school on your right.*

EATON

Eaton is an Anglo-Saxon name meaning eye town: island town, or island of the marsh. The small village has traditional black and white thatched cottages intermingled with modern houses. It is set on the side of a hill amid an abundance of springs which served the villagers into the late 1930s. The hill itself was surrounded by wetland which has since been drained over the centuries to form arable fields.

At the road junction, cross the road and turn left along Lower Lane. Continue as far as the post box and Parish notice board on your right. Stop for a moment by the board. *There is a notice at the top left corner about the village stocks.* Carry on uphill from here and you will see the standing stone indicating the site of the stocks. At the cross roads beware of the traffic and cross the road to Sapling Lane. *On your left is the new stone cross built upon its own raised island where an older cross was reputed to have stood. This was the spot for the May day celebrations but because of the traffic these have been moved to the grounds of the new school.*

Eaton Village Cross

59

THE ROMAN VILLA

Carry on up Sapling Lane. When you reach the top of the hill go past the thatched cottage to your right and look for a white farm gate on your right between an evergreen tree and a farm building. *This is Eaton Cottage Farm. The Roman villa is behind the farm (see Access).*

THE VILLA

Excavated between 1980-82, the villa was the first to be found in Cheshire. Originally the villa, a single storey building of sandstone walls, had a roof of sandstone shingles and clay tiles. It was probably built about AD 170-200. At a later date it was rebuilt incorporating additional living quarters. The strengthening of the walls suggest that an upper story was added to the range.

The villa occupies a prominent position, sheltered from the north and facing southeast to the views over the Cheshire plain, and had a permanent water supply from the natural springs on the hillside nearby. It lies six kilometres from the important Chester to Northwich Roman road. Like many Roman villas, Eaton was probably the main building of a large farming estate and further buildings may lie under the present village. The farm would have grown crops, such as oats and barley, as well as keeping animals. The bones of cattle, sheep, horses and pigs were all found during excavation.

Eaton Villa was different from other farms nearby because it was built of stone and in a Roman style. The owner may have been a local farmer who had grown wealthy under Roman rule and who wished to copy the Roman style of living. Alternatively, the farm may have been bought by a retired Roman soldier with his discharge money. The soldier may have decided to settle in Cheshire after marrying a local woman.

There were also other villas like Eaton in west and south Cheshire. The great fortress at Deva (Chester) brought important benefits to the area. The garrison created a market not only for foodstuffs from farms like Eaton but also industrial items like pottery and metalwork. Important workshops have been identified at Northwich and Wilderspool, near Warrington. Salt was already being produced at Salinae (Middlewich) and Condate (Northwich). The presence of the garrison also controlled unrest among local tribes, bringing peace and stability to the area.

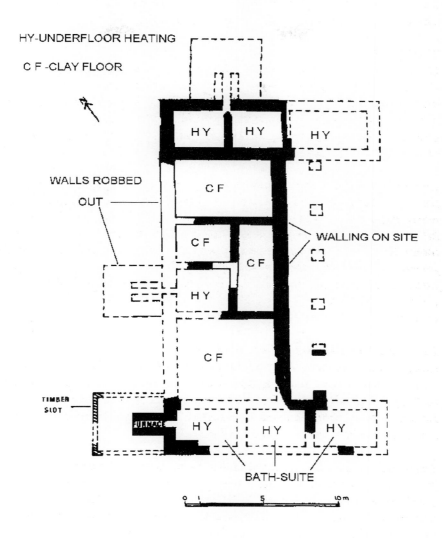

Plan of the Roman Villa at Eaton

Remains of the Roman Villa at Eaton

COBBLERS CROSS

Continue past the farm along Sapling Lane. *A fresh spring of water that the Romans would have used in their villa now comes out onto the lane and walkers still drink from it.* In a short distance you will come to an old track on your left signposted 'Cobblers Cross' and 'Tarporley'. Turn left and continue uphill.

This track originally was a driveway from Arderne Hall to Sapling Lane. Halfway up the hill go through a fieldgate onto a narrow surfaced track which takes you up to a golf course. When the surfaced path ends go half-right and continue to the top of the hill. Proceed straight ahead (beware of flying golf balls) and keep the car park on your left.

Here there is another footpath indicator post. Follow the pointer for 'Cobblers Cross'. The surfaced path goes past the north entrance drive of the golf club house and downhill with an embankment that borders the club house grounds on your left. Go past the first path on your left, but turn down the second.

Immediately go half-right to continue down a narrow sandstone paved path and cross the stile at the bottom. Carry on along an access track passing the cottages on your right until you reach the road. This is 'Cobblers Cross': it is the name of the modern road.

TO TARPORLEY

Turn left and go 45 metres along the road and turn right along a footpath signposted 'Tarporley'. In 20 metres go through the small iron gate and continue alongside the wooden fence. *This was a Victorian path from the Arderne Estate. Note the surface of small chippings.* Climb the stile at the far side of the field and walk through a small copse. Turn left when you reach the modern road. Proceed downhill and when you reach the lower part of the road, on the approach to its meeting with the Tarporley High Street, stop for a moment.

Take note of the Fire Station buildings on your right. These are only where appliances are kept. The main offices were on the High Street. The service was started by the Earl of Haddington in 1869. It was the first voluntary fire brigade in the country, and it still functions, manned by men who have full time work, and who provide cover round the clock with modern equipment.
When you reach the High Street turn left along the pavement. In a short distance you will return to the Crown Hotel.
THE END

ROUTE B
Continue alongside the border of trees on your right and eventually through a field gate. From here, turn half-left and walk over the rise of the field, then you will see the stile ahead.

Carry on half-right and climb the next stile, walk straight ahead and pass through a fieldgate. From here go half-left and get over the stile which takes you onto the road. Turn left, and go to page 57.

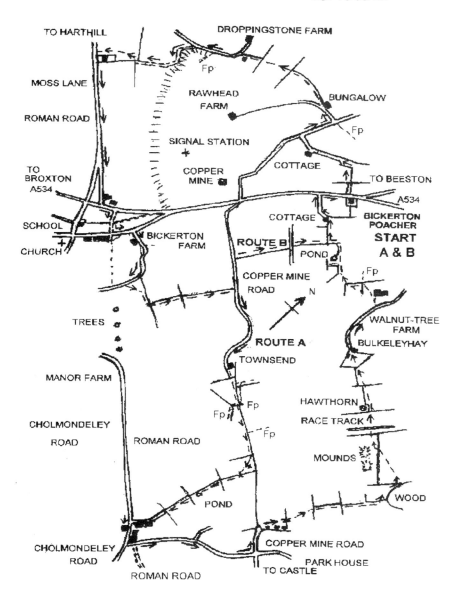

A Roman Road, Medieval Roads and Estate Roads
BICKERTON

START
The Bickerton Poacher Public House SJ 522544

ROUTE A 8 Miles (5 Kms)
This is a walk over the Bickerton Hills through a wooded plantation and along a several medieval roads and a Roman road, returning along the Cholmondeley Estate paths and medieval paths.

ROUTE B 5 Miles (3 Kms)
The shorter walk is over the Bickerton Hills through a wooded plantation and along part of a medieval road and a Roman road, returning along farmworkers' paths.

HOW TO GET THERE
By Car
Car park at The Bickerton Poacher

By Bus
Bus service from Chester to Bunbury

HISTORY
Many Bickerton cottages have been modernised, and new dwellings erected in the village. Farmhouses and their buildings have been converted into private dwellings, the farmlands divided between neighbouring farms. Friesian Holstein cattle are the main breed in this farming area, which gives work to many and their skills are put to good use. Racing and other equine interests flourish around the foot of the hills.

The church nestles between two hills, set within its own walled churchyard, making it a focal point of the village. Work started in the old copper mine in 1697 and continued spasmodically in the 18th and 19th centuries. It was last worked in 1906.

THE BICKERTON POACHER

Walkers are welcome to visit the old inn which may have been a stop for travellers ever since the building was erected in 1642 and sold as an inn 1761 for the grand sum of £64. Look also for the old well near the bar and the old range in the fireplace.

DIRECTIONS

Leave the Bickerton Poacher and cross the main road to the footpath opening in the stone wall. Climb the stile and walk uphill on the enclosed path. Ignoring the stile on your right carry on up through the wood, climb over the railed concrete wall and go along the enclosed track. *This track may have had something to do with the Bickerton Poacher but nothing can be found in any of the old documents of the area.*

When you reach the waymarker post, bear left along the continuation of the track and cross the stile alongside a gate. *Note the views to your left of south Cheshire and the Shropshire hills in the distance.* Go past the cottage on your left and follow the access drive uphill. When the drive reaches the council lane turn right and continue uphill. At the end of the surfaced lane turn left along the entrance drive to Rawhead Farm. *Nowadays, the highest point of Bickerton Hill is the scene of game shoots but in 1981 under drought conditions aerial photographs revealed circular and rectangular features of a possible Neolithic/Bronze Age settlement on the farm land.*

Just past the bungalow on your right, continue ahead along the waymarked footpath. Ignore the kissing gate on your left and carry on downhill. *Note the views from here of north Cheshire and the oil refineries at Elton. Lower down, if you look to your right and slightly back, you will see Beeston Castle in the distance.*

When you reach the open field go straight across heading above the buildings to use a gate ahead. Go alongside the hedge on your right past a wooden shed on your left, through a gate and straight along the access lane of the unusually named Droppingstone Farm. *The name refers to a large rock which has split away from the cliff face to your left.* Proceed downhill ignoring a footpath signpost on your left. *The original entrance track to the farm was on the opposite side of this valley. It ran between Harthill and the farm but later a much improved access was constructed on this side of the valley.*

When you reach the next track, a footpath on your left, go through the walker's gap on the right side of the gate. The track runs through a plantation and just below the Rawhead Hill on your left. The track keeps reasonably level for quite a distance then, at a right bend, it drops sharply downhill. *Look for the Sweet Chestnut trees along here.*

Cross the hidden stile at the lower edge of the plantation. Go half-left across the field to pass the corner of a garden fence on your left. Continue straight downhill and get over the stile that leads onto Moss Lane. Turn left and stop for a moment.

You are now on a Roman road. This road was traced from Huntington (Chester) through Saighton to Milton Green. (See the Milton Green walk.) The road then forded the Golborne Brook and re-aligned southeast where a section is in use as a field access at Clayley Hall Farm. From here it can be traced going uphill as far as 'The Righi' house on the boundary of the Bolesworth Estate. Across the estate it has been obliterated. The road was found again leaving a ford and climbing up to Harthill village and is part of Moss Lane that you are now on.

On the ground above the woods to your left, aerial photography in 1982 revealed crop marks of two phases. The earlier mark was circular with a broad ditch. This being slightly covered by a square ditch enclosure was possibly a Roman Signal Station of two periods or a late Romano-British temple.

BICKERTON

Carry on along the lane. When you reach the fork bear left and stop for a moment. *From this point the Roman road went through the property on your left.* Continue to the main road and stop for a moment. *On the modern OS Maps this main road (A534) is named 'Salters Lane'. Shortly I will show you where the actual salters' lane is.*

Beware of the traffic and cross to the opposite side. Turn left and walk uphill, when you are opposite the house on the other side of the main road, turn right along a grass track. *On reaching the enclosed part of the track you are back on the Roman road. The first section was turned to meet the construction of the A534.*

Soon you will see a stile on your right; continue for two metres and stop for a moment. *There is a track on your left. This was the salters' lane. It crossed the Roman road and continued past the Bickerton School building over the field on your right. Part of it was re-used by the present lane to Brown Knowl village, which you can see beyond the school. From the village it continued straight on across the fields parallel to the modern A534. It was traced as far as Clegg's Hall Farm in Broxton.*

These old tracks became known as salters' roads or lanes because, in the turnpike days, pack animals carried baskets of salt from either Northwich, Middlewich or Nantwich, avoiding turnpike gates to market towns along the Welsh border.

Continue along the Roman road, the road soon widens and slightly bends to your left and then comes to Bickerton Lane. Stop here for a moment. ***The Roman road continued straight across the lane. The field gate that you can see is on the route of the road. The field is private and so we will need to leave the Roman road for a short while.***

Cross Bickerton Lane and turn left uphill. *Note the old quarries on your right and left: sandstone used for the construction of the old properties in the district.* Turn right along Clay Lane, walk past Bickerton Farm on your right and go around the right bend, ignoring the footpath fingerpost on your left. Carry on around a left bend and finally another right bend. Cross the stile on your left and stop for a moment. ***Look half-right to the tall trees that fall in a line across the field. These trees denote the line of the Roman road. On old maps there was a footpath across here but on modern maps the path only starts halfway across. The Roman road beyond the trees goes downhill to become part of the Cholmondeley road. As this is a busy road we shall leave its route and rejoin the Roman road nearer to Cholmondeley Castle.***

MEDIEVAL WAYS

Leave the stile and walk diagonally left across the field until you are walking alongside the hedge and stream on your left. Turn left when you arrive at a footbridge across the stream. Follow the hedge on your left over two fields to a narrow lane.

ROUTE B

Turn left along the lane and cross the first stile on your right. Walk alongside the hedge on your right and then climb the stile onto a farm access track. Turn left and climb a stile on your right, and carry on alongside the hedge on your right. At the far side of the field go through a large gap, turn left and go to page 72.

ROUTE A

Turn right along the lane *You are now on a medieval road which once ran between the Copper Mine and Cholmondeley Castle. Along the lane you will see several timber-framed buildings. Unfortunately some have been modernised but they still contain their original design.* The surfaced lane ends at Townsend Farm. Continue, following the fingerpost to 'Egerton Green'. *On entering the field you can see the old road for a short distance and then it becomes ploughed out.*

Proceed alongside the hedge and ignore the stile on your left, but cross the next stile ahead. In the long field ignore the stiles on right and left but, at the next crossing hedge, go through a field gate. *We shall now leave the route of the medieval road.* Go half-right and keep the steel electric pylon on your left in the middle of the field. *Take note of the field gate to your left in the far corner of the field. This is where the medieval road went, you shall walk a bit more of it later.*

Carry on across a footbridge and turn right. Continue alongside the hedge on your right. *If you see a number of horses on these fields they are race-horses.* Go through a field gate, walk past a pond and go over two stiles onto the field access lane. In a short distance you arrive onto the Cholmondeley Road. *You are now back on the Roman road.* Turn left. Walk along the road as far as the private entrance to Cholmondeley Castle fingerposted to 'Croxton Green.' Turn left and stop for a moment just past the shrubs on your right. *Look at the hilly field on your right and see a road cutting through the hill: this is the Roman road.*

In 1988 I had found a Roman road at Wrenbury-Cum-Frith and traced it back towards Chomondeley Castle and along part of the present southeast entrance to the estate.

Roman Road at Cholmondeley

In early 1990 I received permission from the estate to carry out my search for the Roman road through the grounds. An estimated line from the southeast entrance falls along the road cutting, which was the northwest entrance to the castle grounds.

When the present Cholmondeley/Bickerton road was constructed, a new entrance to the castle was formed on the west side to this new road and the northwest entrance was closed. The present southeast estate drive now terminates at the Cholmondeley/Bickerton road near the Whitchurch (A49) road.

The Roman road was traced a couple of miles further southeast beyond Wrenbury-Cum-Frith where it joined another Roman road going south through Wrenbury. In September 1998 a section of this road was found in an estate southwest of Audlem. The road continued through Norton Hales

70

and Loggerheads (Staffs). Now using footpaths, bridleways and small lanes, the road was traced to Great Bridgeford (Staffs) where it joined a major route that ran between Stoke-on-Trent and Aldridge (Letocetvm).

CHOLMONDELEY CASTLE

The estate covers an area of approximately two square miles. Most of its history is centred around the park and the Cholmondeley family. There are several ways of spelling Cholmondeley which was originally the Saxon 'Calmunds Lea' (a pasture meadow).

The estate played an active part in the first and second World Wars. In the Second World War the castle was used as a naval hospital for shell-shocked sailors. The grounds are open to the public and the gardens display many fine examples of different types of trees.

THE RETURN

It is time to make our return journey. Carry on along the entrance drive around a right bend. Ignore the driveway on your left and carry on around a left bend. When you reach a large sign on your right saying 'Castle Goods Entrance' turn left along a track, *You are now back on the copper mine road for a short distance.* Walk along the edge of the trees and cross the stile on your right. Then walk alongside the large trees on your right.

From the last tree go half-left and cross a footbridge. Proceed straight ahead to the top of the hilly field. When you have reached the top, stop. *Ahead and below, you can see what was once called the Cholmondeley Marsh: a low area which spreads from left to right. This has been drained and cultivated over the years and the water collected now forms the meres of the estate.*

Carry on straight downhill to climb a stile on the left side of a field gate. Continue along a made-up track across the old marsh towards two gates ahead. Go over the stile on the right of the gates and alongside the hedge on your left. At the edge of a wood go through the gate on your left and walk alongside the wood on your right. Follow the curve of the wood and climb the next stile.

Follow the fingerpost waymarked to 'Bulkeley' across the field. On your left you will see two, large tree-topped grassy mounds. Walk towards the lower end of the one farthest away from you. Soon you will see a water trough and in a few metres more, cross the stile on your left in the wire fence. Turn half-right and go through the field gate ahead.

THE PECKFORTON ROAD
You are now on what was another medieval road. This once ran from the estate through the Peckforton Pass to Tattenhall (see the Beeston Walk).

Continue straight on. (Beware of race horses when crossing this field, you will need to walk across the race track.) Head for a lone tall Hawthorn bush and cross the bridge alongside. Carry on alongside the brook on your left and climb a stile in the far corner of the field. Take the stile by the gate on your left. Proceed half-right and walk uphill to a field gate between a haybarn and a house. *You are still on the medieval road.*

The road now becomes surfaced. When you reach the double white field gates on the left side of a right bend in the road, cross the unmarked stile by the first gate. *You are now leaving the medieval road.* Keep the farm building on your right and from the far corner of the building cross to the distant corner of the field. Ignore the stile ahead but cross the stile on your left. Continue alongside the hedge on your right and climb the next stile. Carry on half-right uphill; when you reach the upper part of the field keep a wire fence on your left.

TO THE BICKERTON POACHER
When you see a large tree-lined pond ahead leave the fence and cross the field keeping the pond, in an old sandpit, on your left. *On a clear day look right for the radiotelescope at Jodrell Bank in the distance.* Continue downhill alongside a hedge on your left and cross the stile. Turn left and, when you reach the field corner, turn right.

ROUTE B joins here
Walk downhill alongside the hedge on your left. Lower down, the hedge becomes a cottage boundary. You need to climb the stile on your left beyond the cottage at the bottom of the field. Turn right, cross a footbridge, turn left and climb the stile on your left. Turn right along the drive to the main road. Turn right and in a short distance you reach the Bickerton Poacher.
THE END

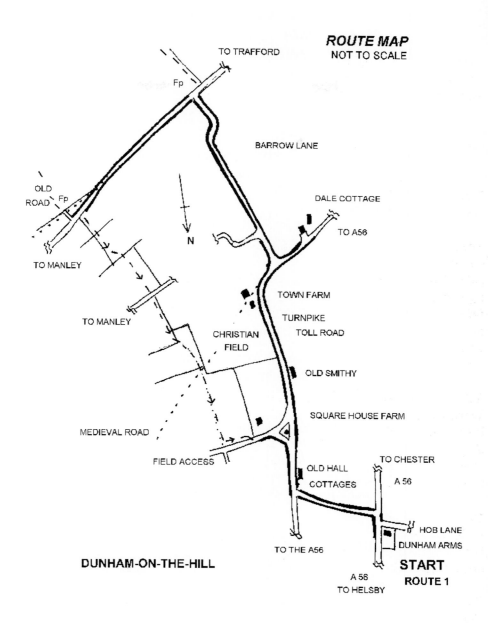

ROUTE MAP
NOT TO SCALE

TO TRAFFORD

Fp

BARROW LANE

OLD ROAD Fp

DALE COTTAGE

TO A56

TO MANLEY

N

TOWN FARM

TO MANLEY

TURNPIKE
TOLL ROAD

CHRISTIAN
FIELD

OLD SMITHY

SQUARE HOUSE FARM

MEDIEVAL ROAD

FIELD ACCESS

TO CHESTER

OLD HALL
COTTAGES

A 56

HOB LANE

DUNHAM ARMS

TO THE A56

DUNHAM-ON-THE-HILL

START
ROUTE 1

A 56
TO HELSBY

73

Turnpike, Salters' & Medieval Roads
including a Monks' Path
DUNHAM-ON-THE-HILL

START
Dunham Arms SJ 471728

ROUTE 1   3 Miles (4 Kms)
This is a short walk along a turnpike and several medieval lanes, and along re-routed right-of-ways across the Dunham fields.

ROUTE 2   4 Miles (6 Kms)
The second walk is along a lost mill lane and a monks' path, and over meadows near to a closed medieval road.

HOW TO GET THERE
By Car
Parking is available at the Dunham Arms, by request, on the A56.

By Bus
Bus service between Chester and Warrington which stops by the inn.
If you intend to do both walks why not take lunch at the pub as well.

HISTORY
Dunham Hill is a small village situated between Mickle Trafford and Helsby. The word 'DUN' is usually seen as a Celtic place name indicating a hill fort. Even in the lowlands people built enclosed settlements on high points for preference, and Dunham is a fine example of one of these villages. There are many houses in the village providing admirable views across the Cheshire plain.

DIRECTIONS ROUTE 1 & 2
Turn right from the inn along the pavement of the A56. Carefully cross the main road to walk up the lane diagonally opposite Hob Lane. When you reach the village road stop for a moment.

This was the old Chester to Warrington road and in 1786 it was re-used for a turnpike. The gradient of the toll road was decreased by cutting through sandstone rock at its entrance and exit from the village.

ROUTE 2 Go to the opposite pavement, turn left and go to page 82.

ROUTE 1
Turn right along the pavement. *Look to your immediate right and the plaque on the first cottage which says "Old Hall Cottages". These replaced the old Dunham Hall which was destroyed by fire during the nineteenth century. All that remains of the hall is the entrance of wide sandstone steps and a worn sandstone gate post (the entrance is between the first cottage and the lane that you have just walked up.)* Continue along the road. *You soon come to a small black building which was the village blacksmith's workshop. The smithy's history gave a clue to a lost medieval road which I will tell you about later.*

Proceed onward. *Look for Rock Farm on the opposite side of the road: house and buildings are upon a foundation of sandstone rock which is clearly visible. Opposite is the old school on your right, which is now the village hall.* When you reach Town Farm on your left go around the right bend. Ignore Barrow lane for the moment and continue down Lowhill Lane. After passing the rocky outcrop, stop for a moment just past the small garage on your left.

If you look to the rear of this building you will see a hollow which has been cut deep and goes beyond the rear of Dale Cottage. This is the way the turnpike descended from the village. It is now re-used as a garden feature. (For further information about the turnpike see 'THE STREET'.)

Go back uphill and turn right along Barrow Lane. Ignore Manley Lane on your left. Carry on along the lane. *Take note of where the run of the lane is situated, on ground that falls away either side, to facilitate surface drainage. The lane was constructed at the time of the turnpike to replace an earlier track that went to Barrow.*

Lower downhill, walk around a sharp right and left bend and meet with the Manley/Ashton lane. Stop for a moment. *Look to your right and to the footpath sign on the opposite side. This footpath was once directly opposite the Barrow Lane end. In 1850 construction of the Chester to Warrington*

75

railway brought about more improvements to the existing road system. Parts of the turnpike were closed off and narrower lanes went out of use leaving only the right-of-ways. The Barrow lane that you just walked from Dunham village was one of the casualties. Other alterations included the Manley/Ashton lane on which you now stand.

There were two major changes to Manley/Ashton lane. Look on the OS map to see the first change: the lane once went in a straight line across fields to join the old Chester road near Bridge Trafford. The railway cut through the route and the lane was re-routed to the Morley Railway Bridge.

Turn left and walk along the Manley/Ashton lane as far as the footpath indicated on your right. Turn right into a track, do not go through the fieldgate ahead, but stop for a moment.

The second change: look to the ditch and hedge that runs away from you on the left side of the fieldgate. These were once alongside the older Manley lane, a salters' road which had been re-used in the early 19th century for the movement of sandstone from Manley Quarry. Aerial photographs proved its existence as it went in a straight line, due east, across the fields to pass to the northeast side of Manley Hall and then, further on, it disappears under the railway by Manley Quarry.

THE SALTERS' ROAD
In 1989 Charles Harston and I excavated the remains of the old Manley lane on the Bridge Trafford side of the railway which revealed some interesting facts about its history.

EXCAVATION REPORT
Removal of the top soil showed a layer of sandstone waste to a depth of 130mm and 9.14 metres wide, ditch centre to ditch centre. A kerbing was formed of a 300mm x 150mm block of hard red clay. Beneath this, there was a layer of soft grey clay of 8.5m x 130mm. This grey clay was laid over another road surface of hard red clay, which had been much narrower, and the ditch on the south side had been filled with soft grey clay and hard stones. This road was 4.8m from ditch to ditch and two wheel ruts 2.1m wide had been filled with stones. On the northern ditch, inner shoulder and in the clay, a flint arrow head was found.

Salters' Road

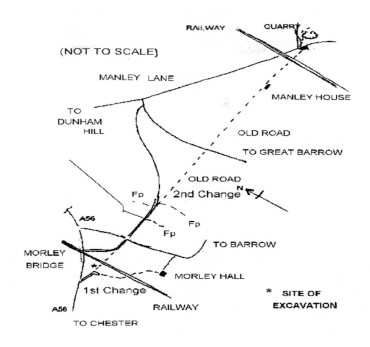

(NOT TO SCALE)

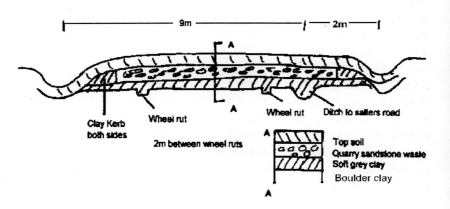

Section of Salters' Road   **Morley/Ashton Lane**

Conclusion

The narrow lower road on the natural red clay was probably used by the salters on their way to Chester. The wheel ruts are somewhat of a puzzle. There was no agger (camber of stones used on Roman roads) and the width was the same as that of other salters' roads found in Cheshire. The flint arrow head was too deep to come from any quarry waste, suggesting a very early use. The upper road was probably early 19th century and was used to carry sandstone from the Manley Quarry to Chester.

TO DUNHAM-ON-THE-HILL

Turn around and go back onto the modern lane. Turn left, and immediately turn right and cross the footbridge and stile. Proceed across the field alongside the wire fence on your right. Go over the next stile and footbridge and continue alongside the hedge on your right.

When you reach the gorse hedge, veer slightly left and cross the stile and footbridge which is near a fieldgate. From here carry on half-left and cross another stile and footbridge. Proceed across the field and take the stile alongside a fieldgate which leads onto the 1786 Dunham/Manley lane.

Go through the fieldgate opposite and walk alongside the hedge on your left, and cross the stile at the field corner of the field. (Ignore the white arrow.) Carry on diagonally to the next gateway and stile but stop for a moment when you are half-way across this field.

Look to your left at the dump which lies between the electric pylon and the left field hedge. This is all that remains of the older Barrow track which was replaced by the Barrow lane that you walked previously from Dunham. The public right-of-way still exists but it has been moved to the fields that you have just walked from the Manley/Ashton lane.

MEDIEVAL ROAD

Stop in the next field for a moment. *From the gap in the hedge on your left between the fieldgate and the corner of the hedge that runs uphill, look uphill to Town Farm cattle shed. Now look in the opposite direction to your right, to the electric pylon at the lower end of this field. Between these points there was once a medieval road here before the turnpike which went to Alvanley.*

78

HOW IT WAS FOUND

Clue one: In the early 18th century two highwaymen robbed the Dunham village post boy on his way to Alvanley. Unfortunately these robbers used the Dunham smithy. The smithy had their own brand mark on the horseshoes. These marks were found at the scene of the crime on that day. Robbers in those days were often hanged on the site of their crime. The field where they were hanged was called Gallows Field. Sometime between 1780 and 1886 the field was renamed 'Christian Field'. This is the field between the hedge on your left and Town Farm.

Clue Two: In 1886 a farmer was murdered on a public footpath which passed through Christian Field. There is no footpath here today, although several of the older residents of the village can remember it being there in their youth.

In conclusion: After the construction of the Chester to Warrington turnpike, only the right-of-way existed.

Clue three: Aerial photographs showed a track from the gap and going towards the electric pylon, at the lowest part of the field, to your right.

CONCLUSION

The medieval road branched from the village road by Town Farm and went across the meadows to Alvanley village and was closed down. I have traced this old road throughout. It once ran close to old farms which are now only shadows in the ground, as shown on aerial photographs.

OLD HAPSFORD LANE

If you look ahead, the ground is disturbed: aerial photographs show a track going north. Beyond the far hedge part of that track is still there today.
It goes towards the rear of Dunham Hill Farm where, on the aerial photographs, can be seen the outline of a building under the ground to the south side of the track. If an estimated line of this track is continued, it falls along the present Hapsford Lane.

Continue straight across the field towards what looks like a stile on the opposite side. When you reach here **do not get over. This is not a stile**. Turn left and walk alongside the field hedge on your right, this is the public footpath.

When you reach the fieldgate on your right, at the top of the field by the farmhouse, stop for a moment. *Now look back to where you crossed the field and you will clearly see the outline of the old Hapsford road.*

The Route of the old Hapsford Road

Proceed through the fieldgate and go onto an access track and stop for a moment. *This track connected the centre of the village with the old Alvanley road and was probably constructed sometime after 1850. In this period, the Chester to Warrington railway had arrived and the A56 road improvements took place. Exactly when the old medieval Alvanley road was finally closed is impossible to date, but another clue given in the history of Dunham mentions that the road was not there in 1889.*

Turn left and continue up the lane taking the right fork. *On your left you will see the old village pump which was the sole water supply for the village before the coming of the main supply in 1916.* Turn right along the pavement of the village road. A left turn will take you back to the Dunham Arms.
THE END

(If you have time and want to walk Route 2 do not turn left, unless you want a break at the Dunham Arms, go straight on)

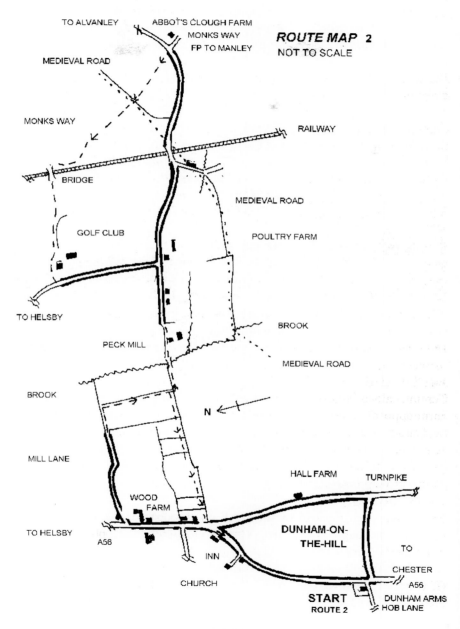

TO ALVANLEY

ABBOT'S CLOUGH FARM

MONKS WAY

FP TO MANLEY

ROUTE MAP 2
NOT TO SCALE

MEDIEVAL ROAD

MONKS WAY

RAILWAY

BRIDGE

MEDIEVAL ROAD

GOLF CLUB

POULTRY FARM

TO HELSBY

BROOK

PECK MILL

MEDIEVAL ROAD

BROOK

N

MILL LANE

HALL FARM

TURNPIKE

WOOD FARM

DUNHAM-ON-THE-HILL

TO HELSBY

A56

TO

INN

CHESTER

A56

CHURCH

START
ROUTE 2

DUNHAM ARMS
HOB LANE

ROUTE 2

Walk past the new school and go downhill. *The large sandstone entrance on your right is Dunham Hill Farmhouse. There is a sign on the a roadside barn saying "Dunham Hall". The protruding porch has the date 1696 and the door inside is studded - in fact the studs are as 'dead as a doornail'.*

The original Dunham Hall was at the summit of the hill and was destroyed by a fire in the early nineteenth century.

Continue to the bottom of the hill to where the old turnpike joins the A56. Beware of the traffic and cross to the opposite pavement. Stop for a moment. *You are standing approximately on the site of the old Wheatsheaf coaching inn which once stood alongside the turnpike. It was knocked down to make way for road widening of the A56, the present Wheatsheaf being built to replace the older one.*

Turn right along the pavement and when you reach Talbot Road, stop for a moment. *To your right and on the opposite side of the main road is a cottage, built over the remains of another coaching inn: The Legs of Man. Look along the A56 to the farm on your left. At the time of the turnpike there was a track which branched from where you are standing and went at an angle past the rear of the farm buildings. This was the old Hapsford lane. In 1844 road improvements turned the lane beyond the farm to meet the A56.*

MILL LANE

Continue along the pavement and, when you have passed the entrance to Wood Farm opposite, beware of the traffic and cross to that side. Walk as far as the fieldgate by a small old brick barn. Turn right and go through the gate, this a public right-of-way: a bridleway. *The track was the original access lane to Peck Mill, which you will see a little later.* Go through a second gate and proceed straight along the track.

When you reach the end of the track go through the fieldgate and continue alongside the hedge on your left. When you reach the crossing hedge turn right and carry on alongside the hedge on your left. At the far end of this field go through the small latch gate and turn left. Stop for a moment when you reach the brow of a hollow.

THE ROMANS ?

Written in a book on the history of Dunham-on-the-Hill there is a statement which says that a Roman road came this way going to Alvanley. The only reason why it is thought to be a Roman road is because in 1889 a Roman gold statue and some Roman coins were found two fields to your right.
I can prove to you that this path is of a much later date and it could not have been a Roman road.

Look ahead to the present brook and beyond to the buildings of Peck Mill. The brook and the mill were all constructed in the same period: approximately the early nineteenth century. The earlier brook was much wider and not contained as the present one. You are standing on the bank of the older brook, a part which had been very wide.

Roman roads or other roads do not ford a waterway at a deep wide section. They use a wide shallow section, unless there is no other option, then a raised causeway would be constructed from stones.

Was there a Roman road two fields to your right? There was a road, but not of the Roman period. It was a medieval road between Alvanley and Dunham Hill. It crossed the stream at a narrow point. The road is older than the mill and its course across the fields has been ploughed out. It ran in the centre of the field between you and the electric pylon that you can see to your right. Where did the Roman finds come from? It is likely that these fell off a cart or from a sack that someone was carrying along this old road. The place where they were found was very close to the ford.

There are other ideas that there may have been a Roman building on the field, although there is no evidence to be seen on the aerial photographs for this side of the brook. There was a building, but this was three fields away on the opposite side of the brook, and its shadow certainly does not indicate a building from the Roman period. Further along the walk I will point out the old road again and you will see it more clearly.

PECKMILL

Continue and go through a small gate onto the concrete bridge across the present brook and pause. *Look over the left side for here are remains of sandstone blocks which can be seen in the stream bed. Before the concrete bridge there had been a sandstone bridge which probably collapsed through lack of maintenance.*

Cross the stile and follow the waymarkers past the barn and Peck Mill House. *The mill is private property, so please do not wander away from the path.* Proceed straight along the entrance drive and go through the gate onto the access lane.

Carry on along the lane ignoring the lane on your left, and go past the poultry farm on your right. Continue around the right bend and where the lane bends left, turn into an access track on your right, and walk past the green barn on your left as far as the fieldgate by a flat bridge over the brook. *From here-on it is private land. Please do not enter.*

On your right there is fieldgate, chained and padlocked, which leads into a narrow field. Look at the hedge which divides the narrow field from the larger field. This hedge was the outer hedge to the old road. I excavated a trench here in 1994, between the trees that you can see further along the hedge. This section indicates the width of the old road. The road forded the brook on your right. It then ran under the access lane and under the nearest end of the green barn.

EXCAVATION REPORT
The road was approximately eight metres wide with a light covering of vegetation and soil. This was removed and revealed a shallow layer of small stones on a yellow/orange base clay. There were large flat stones on the ditch shoulder, south side, but not in any sort of kerb formation. A black silt was removed from the ditch, down to the natural clay. A trench was cut across the road away from the left hedge to reveal the termination of the road stone, but no ditch. Test trenches were excavated further away from the main trench but still no ditch. On the central road surface, two pieces of medieval pottery were found.

Conclusion
It is obvious that this road is not Roman. It was poorly constructed. The road stones had just been thrown down onto a clay surface. The left ditch may be of a later period, because between here and Peck Mill Brook there are places where there is no ditch. The type of construction is similar to that of other medieval roads in Cheshire. The road can be traced from Town Farm at Dunham-on-the-Hill to terminate in the grounds of Rose Cottage at Alvanley.

Medieval Road

TO ALVANLEY

Walk back along the access track to the lane and turn right and go to the uppermost part of the railway bridge. *Look over the left parapet to the rusted rail lines below. This was a branch line between Helsby and Mouldsworth constructed in 1863. Look along the lane and to your left to the access that goes uphill alongside a field hedge. This was the medieval road; the shorter section to the track which returns to the lane is of a much later period, put in when the railway was laid.*

THE MONKS' WAY

Continue over the railway bridge and downhill around the right and left bend. Cross the stile on your left which is directly opposite the access drive to a bungalow: part of Abbot's Clough Farm. *You are now on a monks' way. Narrow paths were constructed by monks to enable them to travel between monasteries. This path was found to run between the monastery at Stanlow*

Point and Manley Hill where it divided into several more paths. The paths were usually cobbled with an edging kerb and no more than 1 metre wide. Nowadays these cobbled paths have been ploughed out and only the right-of-way exists.

THE RETURN

It is time to make our return. Carry on, veer left across the field to climb over the next stile and footbridge. Stop here for a moment. *You now on the remains of the old Alvanley road and it can be seen going up to the crest of the hill alongside the hedge on your right. Please do not leave the footpath, the old road does not carry the public right-of-way status.*

GUNHILL

At the top of the hill, to your right, there is a hedge which runs across the brow. On the field beyond there are stone foundations. During the last world war there were several anti-aircraft guns sited there. The medieval road is still present near the gun site alongside a hedge. It can be traced through a hollow on the other side of this hill and then it continues uphill to pass through Church House Farm at Alvanley. It then crossed the Alvanley/Tarvin road and through the grounds of Rose Cottage Nursery. Its final destination was to meet with the old Alvanley Commonside Lane. Note: not the present Commonside Lane. (See the Helsby/Alvanley walk.)
Carry on straight across the field ahead and when you reach the railway fence turn right. Soon you will reach a stone bridge across the railway. Turn left, cross the stile, taking note of the signs concerning the Helsby Golf Course that you are now about to cross. Follow the waymarkers which keep you on the monks' way. At the car park keep the bungalow on your left and exit onto a council lane. Turn left to the junction of Peck Mill Lane. Turn right and go back the way you came past the mill.

When you have returned across the millbrook and through the small gate on your right, turn left and stay alongside the hedge on your left. Carry on to cross five stiles and, at the sixth, you arrive at the A56. Beware of the traffic, cross the road to the opposite pavement and turn left. *Just past the present Wheatsheaf Inn is the entrance to St Luke's Church built in 1861 for £800.* Carry on along the pavement and around the left bend and you will soon be back at the Dunham Arms.

THE END

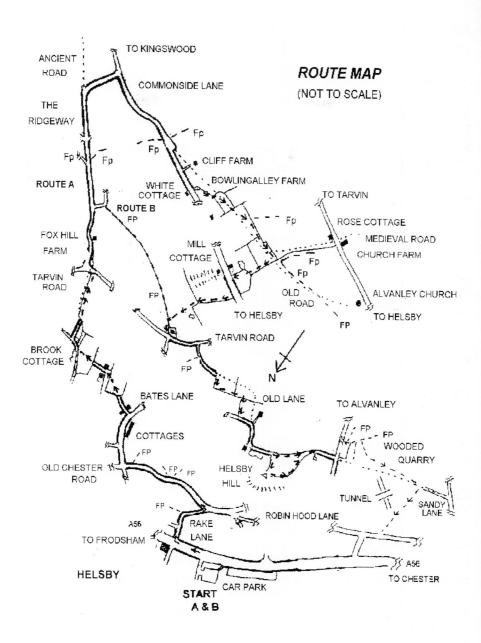

ROUTE MAP
(NOT TO SCALE)

TO KINGSWOOD

ANCIENT ROAD

COMMONSIDE LANE

THE RIDGEWAY

Fp

Fp

Fp

Fp

CLIFF FARM

ROUTE A

WHITE COTTAGE

BOWLINGALLEY FARM

ROUTE B
FP

TO TARVIN

ROSE COTTAGE

MEDIEVAL ROAD

FOX HILL FARM

MILL COTTAGE

Fp

CHURCH FARM

TARVIN ROAD

FP

Fp

Fp

OLD ROAD

ALVANLEY CHURCH

TO HELSBY

TO HELSBY

FP

BROOK COTTAGE

TARVIN ROAD

FP

N

BATES LANE

OLD LANE

TO ALVANLEY

FP

FP

WOODED QUARRY

COTTAGES

FP

OLD CHESTER ROAD

FP

FP

HELSBY HILL

TUNNEL

SANDY LANE

FP

ROBIN HOOD LANE

A56

RAKE LANE

TO FRODSHAM

HELSBY

CAR PARK

A56

TO CHESTER

START A & B

87

Medieval & Prehistoric Lanes
HELSBY & ALVANLEY

START
Station Road, Helsby SJ 491758

ROUTE A   6 Miles (9 Kms)
This is a walk along the Helsby lanes across fields to join a prehistoric track, along a medieval road across the Alvanley fields and over the early quarry roads of Helsby Hill.

ROUTE B   3 Miles (5 Kms)
The shorter walk is across fields to join a section of a prehistoric track, along an old road cut off by a turnpike, and over old quarry roads of Helsby Hill.

By Car
Car Park at Station Road, Helsby.

By Bus
Bus service between Chester and Warrington.

HISTORY
Helsby Hill is a rocky sandstone peninsula which stands above the Cheshire plains overlooking the old bay of the River Mersey. Iron Age tribesmen built a hill fort on the top of the hill and marked a northern frontier of their tribal territory. About 900 AD a Norseman named Toki sailed from Ireland and settled in the Wirral with his followers and family. A frontier settlement was built on the east side of Helsby at the base of the hill above the level of the undrained marsh land. They called it 'Hjallr-by' (the village on the ledge).

DIRECTIONS
Leave the car park and go onto the pavement of the A56 (1786 turnpike) and turn left. Go as far as the Railway Inn, beware of the traffic and cross the main road to enter Rake Lane opposite. Proceed uphill and around the right bend. When you reach the road junction turn left. *You are now on the old Chester to Warrington road which was in use before the turnpike in 1786. In those days there were no trees on the slopes of Helsby Hill on your right. The road here was named "The Sands" due to the continual fall of debris from the hillside.*

Continue uphill passing old and new properties. When you reach the top of the climb, the road widens out for a short distance and narrows again on its descent. On reaching the cross roads, turn right into Bates Lane. Carry on along this lane and around the right bend. Just past the row of cottages on your right, turn left through a small gate onto a public footpath which runs between the houses.

Cross the stile at the end of the path and go slightly left to climb the stile on the far side of the field. Cross the plank bridge and access the footpath which is between a copper beech hedge and privet hedge. At the end of this path go over a planked bridge and another stile, and then continue straight ahead to climb a stile which takes you onto a narrow lane. Turn right and walk across the bridge over the brook. Go as far as the end of the white cottage on your right (Brook Cottage) and turn right into another track. *Glance left to see a pagoda summer house.* When you have crossed the wooden planked bridge over the same brook, stop for a moment. *The narrow lane that you walked before Brook Cottage was prehistoric. This continued through the hills towards Kingsley. Several Stone Age settlements have been found near this ancient track. The track to this bridge was also a prehistoric road. The old road did not cross the stream but ran along the left side the brook. The right-of-way has been re-routed to where it is today.*

THE RIDGEWAY

Continue along the edge of the field keeping the brook on your left. After crossing the stile that leads onto the Frodsham/Tarvin turnpike, stop for a moment. *Look ahead to the farm across the fields. The prehistoric track ran along the left side of the brook going across the fields beyond and to your left of the farm. Here the track becomes part of the road known as The Ridgeway. It was once a two metre wide stone track that ran down from the hills to the old sea coast below Helsby Hill.*

Turn left and then turn right along the modern part of The Ridgeway. Go past Fox Hill Farm on your right. Go around the right bend. When you reach Burrows Lane on your right, stop for a moment. *Look along Burrows Lane to the field gate and footpath at the left bend. Remember Bates Lane into which you turned from the old Chester road. This is where it terminated before the construction of the Tarvin turnpike. Today, between the turnpike and here it is only a public right-of-way across the fields.*

89

ROUTE B
Turn right into Burrows Lane and go to page 95.

ROUTE A
Ignore Burrows Lane and proceed uphill along The Ridgeway. Go past the signposted paths on your left and right (part of the Sandstone Trail). Further up the hill the road levels and you can see now why it was called The Ridgeway: the ground falls away either side. Carry on to the right bend and stop for a moment. *Note the small island of trees and shrubs on the left side of the road. Look ahead through the gate. You will see that the early hedge bank of the road continued straight on. In 1988, with permission, I traced this ancient track. It crossed the present Frodsham/Manley Road and climbed over the hill beyond. I eventually lost it in the grounds of the Kingswood Hospital: its general direction was towards Delamere Forest.*

COMMONSIDE LANE
Proceed around the right bend and continue as far as the T-junction with the present Commonside Lane. Stop for a moment. *I say present Commonside Lane because this lane has been altered too. At the road junction look at the large gap in the corner of the hedge on your left. This is where the original Commonside lane went into the woodlands. It may have branched or crossed the earlier Ridgeway somewhere within those wooded grounds. I could not find any evidence in the hills beyond to suggest that the earlier Commonside lane went beyond the old Ridgeway. There was an enclosure on the ground above Kingswood Hospital, but there is not enough evidence here to suggest a road may have gone this way.*

Turn right and walk downhill through the modern road cutting. When you reach the footpath on your left, signposted Sandstone Trail, stop for a moment. *Look at the hedge on your left and slightly beyond the footpath sign, the hedge makes a sharp return to the present lane. This is where the older road went through. Today there is no evidence in the field beyond, but in 1988 there was. It has since been completely ploughed away. The old right-of-way has been moved and soon you will be walking along it.*

Carry on past Cliff Farm on your left. When you reach the white cottage on your right, cross the stile opposite. *This is the moved right-of-way*. Walk alongside the hedge on your left and climb the stile in the corner of the paddock. Stop for a moment.

Look at the large gap in the hedge on your left, this is where the old road came through. Go half-right and get over the next stile. Stop for a moment. *The old road came across this field slightly to your right and continued into the field ahead. You cannot see it, for these fields have been subjected to heavy ploughing removing any evidence: the road stones will have been spread over a wide area.*

Continue half-left along the path outlined in the crops, this leads to another stile across the field. Do not get over this stile, but turn right and walk alongside the hedge on your left. Go through the kissing gate in the corner of the field. *You are now on the original route of the old road.* When the hedge turns sharp left carry on alongside the wire fence. At the end of the fence turn left along the short enclosed path. When you reach the next kissing gate **go through, but go no further.**

From here you can see the path continuing over a rise as if it is going to the church in the distance. Beyond the rise in the field the footpath has been re-routed away from the church, to exit on the Alvanley/Frodsham road. This is about a quarter of a mile to your right of the church. Originally the old right-of-way went through the church grounds to cross the Alvanley/Helsby road.

There have been many recorded Roman small finds in and around Alvanley, coins and cloak fasteners but nothing more substantial that would suggest buildings.

MORE EVIDENCE OF THE EARLY ROAD
Mr Wright, of Church Farm and owner of the field, said that when he was young he can remember his father ploughing the field for the first time. A stone road was revealed crossing this part of the field, The road went to the rear of Alvanley Church.

At that time a local school teacher who had an interest in the history of the village, visited the field with a party of children, to see the stony road. The teacher had said that this was a Roman road and the original Commonside lane from Kingswood going to Ince: a road which was closed down and replaced by the present Commonside Lane.

I have searched through many early newspaper cuttings that refer to Alvanley and could not find any mention of a new road system to replace a track or footpath that went past the church. The only clue that could be found was on the 1945 aerial photographs which showed a distinct line across these fields. I cannot find a scrap of physical evidence of a path or track in the fields beyond the church.

If it was a Roman road then it should have continued past the church. If an estimated line is continued west, it falls along Primrose Lane (Primrose Lane runs west downhill from Alvanley to the A56 at Horn's Mill). There are two clues on Primrose Lane that may indicate the route of the old road. Where the line joins Primrose Lane, there is a sharp bend in the present lane prior to its connection to the Alvanley/Helsby road. Nearer to the A56 the present lane again bends sharply to the main road. If the road had gone straight on here, it would have arrived at the Horn's Mill Ford. (See "THE STREET".)

A MEDIEVAL ROAD

Look to your left and along the fence that goes along that side. *This is a public right-of-way which has been re-routed. It was originally on the left side of the hedge within the grounds of Rose Cottage. Aerial photographs revealed the presence of a branch road from the old Commonside Lane. This branch was in the field behind you. This went through the pastures of Rose Cottage. Parts of the road are still in existence beyond Church Farm. The farm and Rose Cottage are alongside the Alvanley/Tarvin road which is beyond the rising ground to your left (see map).*

THE RETURN

It is time to make the return journey. Go back through the kissing gate, and walk alongside the hedge on your left. Go through another kissing gate keeping alongside the hedge. Pass through the next kissing gate alongside a large pond. Go across two planked footbridges and alongside the hedge on your right. Pass through a very narrow kissing gate onto the present Commonside Lane and stop for a moment.

THE MILL CLUE

The white thatched cottage which is slightly to your right and on the opposite side of the road was once a small mill. The large pond that you passed in the previous field was the mill pool.

Here is another clue that the present Commonside Lane, that you are now on, is of a later construction. The mill was dated to the seventeenth century, therefore, at that time the present Commonside Lane was not there. There was, however, a narrow track that went to Bowlingalley Farm.

Turn left, walk twenty metres and cross the stile on your right. As you walk alongside the hedge on your left; *look to your right and to the deep hollow which runs downhill from the rear of the old thatched cottage. This was where the outfall from the mill fell into the valley. Any evidence of the water channel, in the lower fields, has been completely obliterated by the plough.*

Cross the next stile and, from where the hedge turns left, continue half-left past a waymarker post to cross a planked footbridge and through a kissing gate. Turn left and stop for a moment. *You are now on the old route of Bates Lane which I mentioned previously.*

ROUTE B joins here

Walk the stoned path which goes through another kissing gate onto the Frodsham/Tarvin turnpike. Turn left again and walk uphill past Teuthill House on your right. Go around the left bend and, opposite a farm, turn right onto the signposted footpath to 'Helsby Hill'.

Note the purposely constructed wall along this lane. It is likely that this was originally an access to the farm before the Tarvin turnpike was constructed. The lane can be traced all the way uphill to where it joins with a present lane.

Carry on along this old lane, ignoring a stile on your right. Eventually, around a left bend, cross a stile. Turn right and walk uphill alongside a fence on your right. *You are now leaving the route of the old access lane.* When you reach a crossing hedge turn left and climb the stile ahead. Stop for a moment. *Look left into the hollow. This is where the old track would have been. It followed the hollow uphill and curved right towards a hedge.* Continue for twenty-five metres and turn right through a kissing gate. Proceed alongside the hedge on your right towards a fieldgate ahead. Go over the stile on the right of the gate which takes you onto a lane. Stop for a moment. *The modern OS maps show this lane going downhill to junction with Bates Lane. Originally the lane ran parallel above Bates Lane and joined the old Chester Road.*

Turn left and carry on uphill to the right bend. Stop here for a moment. *Look into the gardens of the house on your left. Lower down and on your right you will see a slight embankment running downhill. On the crest of this, there is a small sandstone wall in two places. This was the route of the access lane.*

Carry on uphill along the lane. Soon you will reach Harmerlake Farm and a fieldgate across the lane ahead. Pass through the walkers' gap on the left side of the gate. Continue along the lane until you reach a point where it becomes hedged on both sides and there are posts across the path with a walkers' gap.

The brave ones can turn right onto a path which takes you to the top of Helsby Hill. *The bylaws here prohibit clothes lines, roundabouts and organ playing as well as water skiing.* When you have arrived at the OS Height Marker go to your left and take the path that goes downhill along the cliff edge. This eventually will take you back onto the old lane.

The not-so-brave can continue straight on down along the shaded lane. This eventually goes down quite steeply through a rock cutting and, still with sandstone walls, through wooded slopes to combine with the cliff edge walk near a modern house on your right.

The old lane now becomes a normal road surface descending rapidly to the Helsby/Alvanley road below. Stop here for a moment. *Two hundred years ago the lane you have just walked down originally went straight across the Alvanley road, but since then it has been destroyed by a quarry. A little later on I will point out the remainder of the old lane.*

Turn left and use the gate into Helsby Quarry Woodland Park on you right. Take the second steps on your right and continue downhill. *A branch to the right once went through a tunnel, this is now closed due to the unstable rock in the roof.*

Go left up some steps and walk down a cutting to a gateway that leads onto Sandy Lane. Do not go through but stop for a moment. *Sandy Lane was the continuation of the old hill lane. Downhill it eventually meets with Rock Lane.*

The Tramway Tunnel

The tunnel was constructed for a quarry tramway that carried sandstone, downhill and across the marshes to Ince Pier. The pier jutted out into the River Mersey and the stone was shipped to Liverpool. The Customs House at Cannings Dock in Liverpool contained much Helsby stone, and it was used extensively in the construction of both Liverpool and Birkenhead Docks.

Turn right, inside the quarry, and continue downhill to the next gate. *Along here you will see the opposite end of the tunnel.* Go through the gate and turn right, then first left to reach the A56. Turn right to the pedestrian crossing and the car park.
THE END

ROUTE B
Walk directly ahead and cross the stile to the right of the fieldgate. *This was a section of Bates Lane that you walked previously. When new road systems were introduced, this section of the lane across the field was closed down leaving only a public right-of-way.*

Continue alongside the brook on your right. Keep straight on until you arrive at a planked bridge and kissing gate on your right then go to page 93.

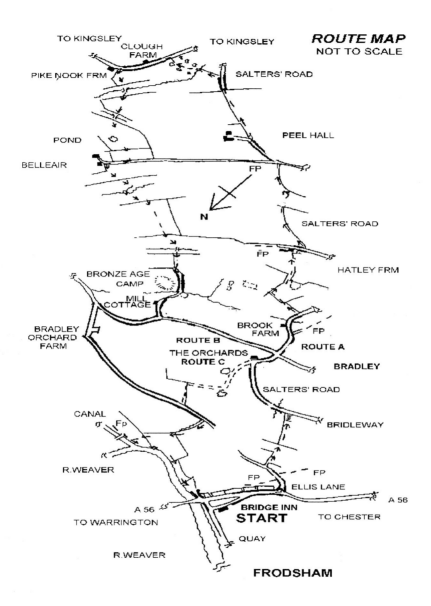

ROUTE MAP
NOT TO SCALE

Salters' & Medieval Roads
Mill Lanes & Quarry Roads
FRODSHAM

START
Bridge Inn by the River Weaver A56 bridge east of the town SJ 529784

ROUTE A   6 Miles (9 Kms)
This is a walk along a salters' road across the medieval landscape of Bradley village, along farmworkers' footpaths and old mill lanes, past a Bronze Age camp and the remains of an old watermill, returning over the meadows alongside the River Weaver. Part of the route can be muddy.

ROUTE B   4 Miles (6 Kms)
This shorter walk goes along a section of a salters' road and a mill lane, returning along a section of the original Catton Hall lane and across the meadows alongside the River Weaver.

ROUTE C   3 Miles (4 Kms)
The shortest walk uses a section of a salters' road and an old quarry road. It goes along a short section of the original Catton Hall lane and across the meadows alongside the River Weaver.

HOW TO GET THERE
By Car
Vehicles can be parked in front of the Bridge Inn or along Quay Road adjacent to the inn.
By Bus
The Chester to Warrington service stops by the Bridge Inn.

HISTORY
Frodsham is situated on the southwest bank of the River Weaver. It emerges into history in Anglo-Saxon times as Froda'sham. This pre-conquest hamlet became the chief village of a large parish embracing Kingsley, Alvanley, Manley and Helsby, indicating a strong possibility that the church at Frodsham was a Monastic Missionary Centre.

97

The Domesday book records that, before 1066, the Manor of Frodsham belonged to the Saxon Earl Edwin of Mercia. The position of the village on the road from Chester to Warrington and the proximity of the river were important assets, and gradually a small but prosperous medieval market town developed. In the 18th century ship and boat building, and a salt refinery were established here. Nowadays the M56 keeps some of the through traffic out of the town.

The A56 Weaver bridge was constructed to replaced a much earlier bridge on the old toll road. The exact location of this older bridge can be placed by looking at the small road in front of the Bridge Inn and then across the river to the Aston Arms and the rows of white cottages, these were once alongside the old Chester road. The older bridge may have been made of wood or a weak type of sandstone, too weak for today's traffic. Look at the riverside to see the remaining abutments. (Daniel Paterson 1811 in his book 'Roman Cheshire' mentions a wooden bridge over the Weaver here.) Bridge Cottages on the new road were built in 1888.

DIRECTIONS
Cross the main road to the pavement opposite and turn right, walk uphill and when you reach Ellis Lane, signposted 'Catton Hall and Kingsley', turn left. Pass the houses on this unadopted road and continue onto a muddy track. Ignore the footpath on your left and one on your right to 'Townfield Lane' and continue for twenty metres. Cross a brook and turn right along a field access. (The public footpath sign keeps getting knocked down.) This access is only a short walk and you will enter an open field where you go alongside the hedge on your left.

Where the hedge turns to your left, proceed straight on, and cross the iron stile ahead. From here carry on alongside the wire fence on your left. Soon you will descend through some trees and down some steep steps, where the path meets with a bridleway. Turn left and walk downhill into a hollow and cross the wooden bridge. *A picnic table on your left supports a variety of carved flora and fauna.* Continue uphill and when you reach the upper fields stop for a moment. ***This was a salters' road. Pack trains similar to the Welsh packhorses carried salt from Northwich and Winsford to the salt refinery which was once on the Frodsham dockside. The refined salt would then be shipped to many parts of the world.***

You are standing on cobble sets. These were embedded between sandstone kerbs either side. One of the kerbs can be seen and the other side lies buried beneath the hedgerow on your right. The width of the old road would have been approximately two metres wide.

Salters' Road

BRADLEY VILLAGE

Carry on along the old road as far as the T junction by an improved barn called 'The Orchards'. The lane on your left signposted 'Frodsham Bridge' originally went to several old clay quarries.

ROUTE C   Turn left and go to page 105.

ROUTE A & B

Turn right and proceed along the lane as far as the cross roads.

ROUTE B   Turn left and go to page 105.

ROUTE A

Go straight on along Watery Lane ahead. *This is the continuation of the salters' road.*

BROOK FARM

Go around the left bend and down into a hollow. Proceed up the opposite side of the lane and around the right bend. *You now have left the route of the salters' road which originally went along the opposite side of the hedge on your left.*

Continue for a short distance and cross the stepped stile on your left; walk alongside the hedge on your right as far as the next stile.

This is where the salters' road crossed your path and continued up the fields to your right. Climb the stile and walk alongside the hedge on your left and follow the waymarkers up the field. When you reach the field access between two wire fences, stop for a moment.

SAXON MILL

Look to your right at the large half-dished shape hollow. This was a reservoir, it has since been part filled in. If you let your eyes follow the natural watercourse from this pool, it goes to your left and down the field on that side. Turn round and look down to the lower part of the field and to where a tree stands on its own. Here there was another and much larger pool, also filled in. A channel from this second pool went towards the trees on the right side of the field, where there is yet another pool. This third pool is on the edge of a deep gutter. The outlet from this empties into the gutter, a third of the way down the outlet there is a very large stone inserted into the side. This may have been a foundation for a small wooden paddle wheel.

Slightly left of the channel and halfway down the gutter side, there is a platform of levelled earth, where a wooden building may have been. It is likely the platform is all that remains of a Saxon Mill. There was a mill recorded in the Domesday Book 'molin ibi hiemale' (it has a winter mill). Two of the pools have been re-used in a later period for watering cattle. In 1989 a mill, like this one, was found near Golly (Wrexham).

The mill would have only been used for making small amounts of butter or cheese, enough to provide for the small settlement which was close by. In the Saxon period, mills were crude structures using green timber from trees in the locality. Wheat and corn was threshed with flails and ground in hand-querns.

Carry on along the field access and climb the stile by the field gate, proceeding towards the Hatley Farm buildings ahead. Cross the stile set in the fence on your right. From here go half-left and around the corner of the farmhouse garden hedge and over the next stile which leads onto the Hatley Farm access drive. Turn right, cross the stile on your left, then go alongside the hedge on your right. *You are now back on the salters' road. There is no evidence of the old road in this part of the field. It only starts to become evident when you are halfway along. On the approach to the next stile, stones have been laid along the road, but these are of a much later date. Nearer the stile, the ground has been disturbed and the old road stone beneath can be seen much more clearly.*

Cross the stile and continue along the stoned access towards the sewage works and poultry sheds. By the hedge, the track and footpath turn left to run parallel with the field boundary on your right. Climb the stile which leads onto the access lane to Peel Hall Farm. Stop here for a moment. *The route of the salters' road originally went straight through the grounds of the sewage works and met with the farm access drive to the right of the field gate, which is on your right.*

PEEL HALL
Proceed straight ahead and along the Peel Hall drive. When the drive bends left cross the stile immediately on your right and then turn left alongside the walled garden. Continue until you are halfway and stop for a moment. *Look over the wall and you will see a hollow which runs from your left to your right: this is the remains of the salters' road. Look towards the hall which stands on a raised mound; the mound is surrounded on all four sides by a moat. A few years ago a colleague used a metal detector in the enclosed gardens of the moated site. The finds were pennies dated from the seventeenth century to the modern small penny. The owner of Peel Hall, Mr Tom Gleave, said that a church fete had been held in his garden every year for as long as he could remember.*

Mr Gleave, during his life-time at the farm, has cleared the moat and stocked it with a species of giant goldfish. Improvements to the farm buildings had revealed the first farmhouse, outside the moat, dated to the sixteenth century. The moat was built around an eighteenth century farmhouse which was smaller in size. The present farmhouse, a much larger design, is from the early nineteenth century.

Peel Hall

PIKE NOOK

Carry on along the path leaving the walled garden and continue alongside a field hedge. Cross the stile which leads down an access into the wooded valley, Pike Nook. Stop for a moment. *Look over the hedge on your left. The original road is immediately below the hedge. It descends into the valley and rejoins the present access lane by the cottage. From here the road went into Kingsley village where it divides into two tracks, one going to Northwich and the other to Nantwich.*

THE RETURN

It is time to make our return journey. Proceed downhill and climb the stile on your left. Go down the path deeper into the valley, get over another stile and cross a footbridge. Walk uphill on the far side and over the stile which leads onto a narrow lane. Turn left and continue downhill past the white buildings of Clough Farm on your right. When the lane bends to your right by Pike Nook Farm cross the stile on your left and follow the path down the field, over the stile by the side of the wooded valley. Cross the footbridge, made from a single slab of sandstone. Continue uphill and climb the stile leading into the open field above.

FARMWORKERS' PATH

Leaving Pike Nook, go half-right across the field and soon you will see a waymarker post on the shoulder of the next wooded vale. Cross the bridge over the stream and climb the stile on the opposite side.

Turn half-left and go across the open field to its highest part. When you are level with the pond on your right, you will see the stile ahead. From this continue straight ahead and get over the stile which leads onto the access lane to Belleair Farm. Turn right. (As you approach the farm, dogs may rush towards you. There is no need to fear, they are only noisy.)

MILL PATH

When you near the farm buildings turn left and climb the stile on the woodland edge. Go down the steps. (Step over a fallen tree.) Ford the stream, proceed up the opposite side and when you are near the top of the bank stop for a moment. *Look to your left and you will see a large water collection pool with its outlet to the stream below.* Cross the stile ahead and go half-right, walk a few more paces and stop for a moment. *Look to your right and you will see another large pool. This pool was linked to the one you first looked at on the valley side. These were watering pools for cattle.*

MILL ROAD

Continue across the field, when you reach halfway and are in sight of the stile ahead, stop for a moment. *Look to the fence which is on your right and much lower down the slope of the field. You will see a dip in the ground surface which runs parallel to and on the opposite side of the fence. This is all that remains of an old road that has been ploughed out.*
It was a mill road running between the large estates near Kingsley and Bradley Beech Mill. Soon you will walk part of the road which, nowadays, is only used for field access.

ROMAN CAMP

Look half-right into the far distance towards Runcorn and the hill that stands to the rear of the rows of white houses which run left to right across the hill face. It was on this hill that the remains of a Roman fort was found under the foundations of the older houses which cover the hill. The Romans had a commanding view for miles around.

103

BRONZE AGE CAMP

Climb the stile ahead and go straight across the field. Soon you will see a marker post indicating the path down into a gutter. Cross the narrow plank bridge and up the steep steps on the opposite side, get over the stepped stile and then go half-right to climb the stile on your right, turn left and stop for a moment. *You are now on the old mill road. Look into the field on your immediate right. There is a raised earth platform halfway down the field. This was a Bronze Age camp which has been described as the smallest hill fort in Cheshire. It had a single curving bank and outer ditch facing the uphill approach. There is no clear indication of an entrance.*

A few metres along the mill road, when you reach a red field gate on your left, stop for a moment. *Look into the field on the other side of the gate. There are several house platforms of various dates. The trees here consist of apple, damson, and black Jacob plum.*

BEECH MILL

Carry on down the mill road. When you reach the wooden bridge over Beech Brook, stop for a moment. *If you look to your left carefully you will see what remains of an old mill pool.* Cross the bridge and stop on the right bend. Look into the large gap on your right. *This was the site of the upper medieval mill of Beech Brook. If you look carefully between the overgrowth you may see some of the remaining stonework of the mill walls.* Go around the bend and up the hill. Pass through the small gate to the left of a padlocked fieldgate. *Beech Mill House, on your right, was the miller's cottage.* Continue uphill and when you reach the council lane turn right.

ROUTE B joins here

LOWER BROOK MILL

Proceed along the lane and around a right bend. Turn left into the first stone track (footpath) on your left and stop here for a moment. *Look further down the council lane and to the yard in the trees on the right. This was the site of the lower medieval mill on Beech Brook. In the past there must have been a good torrent of water in the brook to have supported two mills. Nowadays, the water level has dropped and it is doubtful that one mill could be supported.*

WEAVER MEADOWS

Carry on along the entrance road to Bradley Orchard Farm. When you approach the farm, continue ahead keeping the farmhouse on your right; the route is well waymarked. Beyond the farm buildings climb uphill along a high shoulder of land above the River Weaver meadows. *This was the original Catton Hall road.* Beyond the gates ignore the footpath on your left signposted 'Bradley'.

ROUTE C joins here

RIVERSIDE WALK

Continue straight on uphill along the improved road. When you reach a deep brook and tall hedge on your right, turn right and follow the footpath signpost downhill alongside the brook and across a field. Climb the stile ahead and go onto the path which leads to the River Weaver. Stop for a moment.

To your right are the remains of river locks. These once were used for barges going to upstream to Northwich, but since cutting another canal for much larger boats, these locks have become redundant.

Turn left and proceed along the river bank downstream. (There are times when parts of this path become flooded from the river; there is higher ground to your left and a suitable dry path can be found along this.) Soon you will be able to see the A56 bridge ahead; the path leads onto the A56.
THE END

ROUTE C

Proceed along the old quarry lane. *If you go quietly when approaching the quarries, now filled with water, you will see a number of water fowl.* The lane twists and turns passing close to the quarries then it goes downhill to end at a stile. Cross this and turn left and along the partly ploughed-out lane. Cross the next stile and turn left along Catton Hall lane and go to page 105.

ROUTE B

Follow the modern road and when you reach a footpath sign on your right of a left bend go to page 104.

THE STREET

A Roman Road

Between

Chester (Deva) and Warrington (Wilderspool)

THERE ARE NO PUBLIC FOOTPATHS ALONG THIS ROUTE.

Map References OS 1: 25.000 Pathfinder Series

Permission will be required to enter private land

HISTORY

This monograph sets down the evidence collected by archaeological investigation along the Mickle Trafford to Preston Brook section of what is widely accepted as a Roman road built about AD 70 between the Deva Fortress at Chester and the Roman settlement at Wilderspool (Warrington.) Both Roman road and the old Chester Road shared much of the same route.

The *Street* may have been built around AD 70 from the Deva Fortress (Chester) to the Roman settlement at Wilderspool (Warrington). The route of the eighteen mile road has puzzled historians for over one hundred years.

Ivan Margary, author of **'Roman Roads of Britain'** *stated that he had traced the* **Street** *from Chester as far as Picton Lane at Mickle Trafford and it could be found again at Preston Brook, a gap of some twelve miles.* Mickle Trafford lies approximately three miles northeast of Chester on the A56 Warrington Road. Preston Brook is approximately four miles southwest of Warrington on the same road. It is not known exactly where the *Street* leaves the Deva fortress. *Margary suggested that it branched east from Liverpool Road which leaves the Northgate and went along the present Brook Lane through the Kingsway estate and to Mannings Lane at Newton.*

Chester archaeologists place the *Street* leaving the Eastgate and then immediately northeast along Flookers Brook (Hoole), through Newton Hollows and onto Mannings Lane. This was also the route of the initial Chester to Warrington road. The route was turnpiked in 1786.The answer to the true where-abouts of the Roman road may never be known as housing and industrial development covers this area.

THE STREET SJ 4255/6855

At Mannings Lane the *Street* runs through Hoole Bank village to the north side of Mickle Trafford. The present lane runs on the exact course of the Roman road until it reaches the brow of a hill at Mickle Trafford, where it becomes a cutting down the hill. The road cutting is very overgrown and two bungalows have been built across its path. The next and last sighting of the Roman road is in a field next to Croft Cottages and opposite the junction of Picton Lane. The continuation of the road from this point was difficult to trace, due to the present lane being turned to meet with the (A56) turnpiked road. If the line of the Roman road is continued it would have needed to ford a brook. The course of this brook has been changed and the majority of it has been piped through a large estate. The following field, on line with the Roman road and ford, is of a clay nature, rather hollow and very wet, while aerial photographs remain quite featureless giving no hint or suggestion of any road that may have crossed this field.

MICKLE TRAFFORD

In the winter of 1993/4 British Gas were in the process of placing a second pipe-line through the fields which lie across the assumed line of the Roman road. The hollow field and the following field which is called *The Gibbets* SJ 4468/7030 were being used as a stock pile area for the track vehicles and all the top soil had been removed. An archaeologist of British Gas and I searched for evidence of the *Street* across these two fields. Between the bank of the brook by Picton Lane and the northern hedge of *The Gibbets* there could be seen a light scatter of sandstone chips which were foreign to the natural clay sub-soil of the two fields. (These chips were similar to the ones found on an excavation in 1986 on a section of the *Street* northeast side of Deeside Timber Mills.) Other types of stones were present but these may have been natural, although there were a greater number along the line of the road than in any other part of the fields. There was no evidence of any road ditches in the first field. Across the Gibbets field a northerly ditch was in use and, if there had been a ditch on the southern side, it may have been the thin dark line in the clay. The scatter of sandstone chips disappears under the rear boundary of Deeside Timber Mills. There had been a main gas pipeline inserted across fields in 1964 and nothing was found at that time to prove the existence of the Roman road.

Conclusion : The possible reason that nothing could be found in 1964, was that the pipe was put beneath the ground via a single narrow trench across the fields. The top soil and sub-soils were not separated and therefore any scatter of stones would be mixed in with these soils. The sides of the trench were compressed by heavy machinery and thus would disguise any evidence of ditches. On the southeast side of the suggested road in the Gibbets field there was a spring. With grateful help of the contractors on site this was dredged but nothing of importance came out of the murky waters.

THE PADDOCK SJ 4409/7006

Excavation 1986: small field northeast side of Deeside Timber Mills Mickle Trafford. Aerial photographs show a distinct track parallel to the northern hedge. The general make up of the ground was of a thin top soil on a sticky yellow/brown clay and below this a hard red boulder clay. The area of the excavation contained an old corrugated tin animal shelter in the northwest corner of the paddock. The soil was deeper within the shelter because of continuous animal occupation. A test trench of one metre wide was cut across a ten metre length strip of which the northern end ran through the shelter. A centre line was struck and the southern side excavated first.

The thin top soil was removed to reveal a small spread of sandstone chips and small stones rammed into a hard dark red/yellow clay. There was a wheel rut which ran with the stony surface and it measured 100mm wide and 80mm deep. The surface sloped down slightly, to level off and on this slope there was another wheel rut of the same dimensions. The level surface had a spread of the sandstone chips and stones and next came four fist sized stones in line which formed an edge. Beyond these larger stones there was a sticky black silt which when removed formed a small 'V' of 300mm wide and 150mm depth.

A test trench was excavated one metre beyond this and it was found to be the natural sticky yellow clay and boulder clays. The northern side of centre was excavated down to the chipped surface. Nearer to the animal shelter another wheel rut was found of the same dimensions. The distance from the centre of this rut to the initial rut was one metre; which is the width of Victorian handcarts. Nearer to the shelter a hand made brick foundation was found beneath the framing of the refuge. Inside the shelter the stones and sandstone chips had been removed, being replaced with ash and clinker. It was four metres to the next foundation and on the far side of this was a ditch which had been deepened and was still in use. Outside the shelter a trench was cut through the stoned surface to reveal a spread of small greyish gravels over hard red boulder clay.

Conclusion: It is likely that this was the route of the old Chester road and it has run on the original Roman road. Continuous use, especially the pushing of carts, has destroyed the traces of the Roman surface. It is also plausible that the majority of the road surface was removed and re-used in the construction of the turnpike which is a mere twenty metres to the southeast of the older road. The line of the Roman road runs into and through the garden of the northern end of three cottages. The hedge bordering the old road continued past the north end of Paddock Cottage and terminates in the grounds of Mickle Trafford Trout Farm.

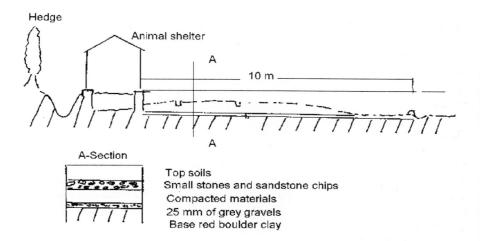

Paddock Field, Mickle Trafford

BRIDGE TRAFFORD

Mr T James, of Mill House, said that when he had landscaped the garden which fronts the A56, he found sandstone chips and other types of stones along the roadside hedge. He traced these along the field side of the hedge until reaching the River Gowy Bridge. At the time he thought that these had something to do with the construction of the A56.

There is no actual evidence of the old road today because the field between Mill House and the river has been used as a landfill site and any remains are well and truly buried. The Roman ford was on the south side of the river bridge, but since the River Authority continually clean out the river there are no remains of this either.

109

The Cheshire County Council Archaeological Department has a record of Roman coins having been found at the site of the ford.

It is my sole assumption that the ford SJ 4492/7110 is not the *Street* ford, but that of another Roman road which went north to Ince (Midden Street as shown on the OS 1837 Map). It was likely that the road went between or under the cottages which are built on the opposite side of the right hand bend of the A56 and continued along several of the straight sections of the present lane to Ince. Test trenches were carried out along Ince Lane in the grounds of Manor Farm and Cross House Farm, but there was no evidence to suggest the existence of a road.

Conclusion: The Roman coins suggest this was a well-used track but there is no archaeological evidence to prove conclusively that the route was a properly constructed Roman road. In 1996 evidence was found of Roman remains near the village of Ince.

THE GOWY
There is only one other place where the *Street* could have crossed the river. The area must be looked at as it was **before the insertions** of the two channels for the mill. It was assumed that all the river meadows between the road bridge and the railway once flooded, but this was not so.

With the help of the River Weaver and River Gowy Water Authority, I found that the area which flooded was between the Morley Channel (northeast side) and the railway embankment. This is indicated by the areas of peat. The land between the modern sluice channel (northwest side) and the Morley Channel did not flood due to it being higher ground and of a natural boulder clay.

Conclusion: The *Street* could have forded the Morley Channel further upstream from the known ford. Lack of present evidence of a ford does not mean there never was a ford. Since Roman coins were found near the A56 road bridge, it has been accepted that this was - **the ford**. Another clue to a second ford was in the Morley Channel itself. Early records of the River Authority pinpoint two sections of the river that were deepened. The first section close to the present bridge and another section SJ 4510/7105 further upstream, may have been the second ford. This section falls on line to the Shrewsbury Arms, and two trees on the southwest river bank and a small terrace, which is on the northeast embankment of the Sandfields Farm fields.

SANDFIELDS FARM
Just prior to this terrace climbing the river bank there was an unusual heap of stones, of a type which are foreign to the river area. The terrace SJ 4535/7115 is only three

110

metres wide and had a dark line of grass which may indicate there was once a ditch here, on one side. There was only a scattering of stones on the surface, but mainly it is quite clean, probably due to most of the stones having been removed. When the terrace reaches level ground it has been ploughed out. No evidence shows on current aerial photographs.

An excavation was carried out at Morley Railway Bridge by Frodsham & District Local History Group who proved the existence of a Roman road. It was assumed that the *Street* lies under the present stretch of the A56 from the railway bridge to the filling station at Dunham-on-the-Hill. If an estimated line is drawn from this section of the A56 back to the River Gowy **it falls onto the terrace on the river bank**. The majority of the field gates are on this line.

There has been too much disturbance across the Sandfield meadows to prove the existence of an old road, although there was a hint of a clue at the junction of the old Manley/Ashton lane to the turnpike.

Conclusion: If the *Street* branched from Midden Street, after the ford by the A56 road bridge, there would need to be a very sharp dog-leg to bring it onto line with the Morley Bridge section. Here is another reason why there had to be another ford.
See Map 1

MORLEY BRIDGE
The railway was constructed in 1850 and the Morley Bridge was built to carry the A56. The old turnpike road (1786) which was cut through by the railway can be seen on the southwest side and fronts several cottages. On the northeast side of the railway and in line with the cottages, in the field known as *Pavement Heys*, there is an agger like feature which lies parallel to the road ramp built for the A56 bridge.

PAVEMENT HEYS
SJ 4610/7165   An excavation in the field known as Pavement Heys was made in 1988 by Frodsham & District Local History Group at Morley Bridge.

A report with Cheshire County Archaeology Department Chester states :

Field at Morley Bridge called 'Pavement Heys' on 1844 Tithe Map. In 1986 Dutton found pebbles in hard clay and possible kerbing stones. Partly overlain by A56 road embankment.

July 1988 Excavation by Frodsham & District Local History Group revealed cambered agger with shallow metalling of hard packed reddish clay with scattering of small pebbles over a layer of sandstone chips, with reddish & yellow clay beneath. The SE slope of the agger was overlain by hard pink clay with three large chunks of sandstone in a clear continuous row. Side ditch to NW of agger was shallow with a fill of blackish clay silt. The outer side of the ditch was banked and formed of orange brown hard clay. Probably a roadside embankment intended to raise main carriageway above flooding risk.

Route probably founded by Romans, but then re-used by medieval turnpike & present A56. Finds were all post medieval. 2 sherds of pottery & metal objects.

CORNHILL

The *Street* lies under the turnpike and the present A56 northeast from Morley Bridge. The 1893 OS Map shows a parish boundary along this length of road. Parish boundaries were usually formed on existing features. The Roman road, the old Chester road and turnpike passed to the rear of the Dunham Hill filling station.

The bypass of the A56 around the hill was constructed in 1844 and widened in 1938. It is on record at Chester Museum that Roman coins and pottery had been found (1888) in the grounds to the rear of the filling station.

DUNHAM-ON-THE-HILL

Dunham Hill is a small hill situated between Mickle Trafford and Helsby. The word 'DUN' is usually seen as a Celtic place name indicating a hill fort. Even in the lowlands people built on high points for preference and Dunham is a fine example of one of these settlements. The Romans would certainly make use of the hill and the long ridge that runs towards Helsby.

NURSERY FIELD

SJ 4685/7220. A test trench was excavated across an agger-like feature on the turnpike road between Dunham Hill Nursery and Dale Cottage, southeast side of the A56. A trench of four metres length was dug and 300mm of a very wet sandy top soil was removed to reveal a layer of large square shaped cobbles set into the red sandy clay. Before the trench could be excavated any deeper, it rapidly filled with water and had to be abandoned. The landowner said that this old road cutting had become a large drain for water from the top of the hill.

THE DALE (Originally Dingle Cottage)

The turnpike cutting goes uphill through natural sandstone rock to the rear of Dale Cottage. There is a shelf of three metres wide on the southeast side of this cutting and then a hedged embankment of one metre high edging the fields. A trench was cut across this shelf to reveal a sub-soil mixed with sandstone chips, small pebble stones and reddish brown clay. A test trench in the field side of the garden revealed the presence of the stones and chips near to the hedge. Further out into the field there was too much disturbance to warrant a worthwhile search.

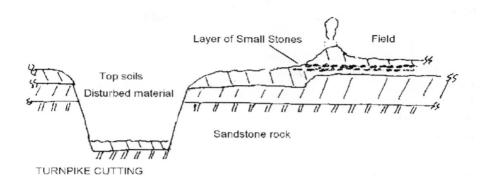

TURNPIKE CUTTING

Rear Garden of Dale Cottage, Dunham-on-the-Hill

An estimated line from the rear of the filling station to the shelf goes across Lowhill Lane and to the rear of the old village school. It then falls onto the turnpike by the village well. The turnpike from Dale Cottage turned east uphill and became the upper part of Lowhill Lane by Townfield Farm and it used the present village road. The turnpike from the uppermost part of the village runs downhill through a deep cutting in the natural rock It can only be assumed that the *Street* was destroyed by the turnpike from the brow of the hill down to the modern A56. **See Map 2**

THE WHEATSHEAF INN
An early Wheatsheaf Inn stood alongside the old Chester road/turnpike on this side of Dunham Hill. In 1844 the A56 bypass was constructed, cutting the inn off from the turnpike. In 1938 the A56 was widened and the inn was demolished then rebuilt where it stands today.

HIGHFIELD NURSERY COTTAGE FARM
Opposite the Wheatsheaf Inn and on the southern side of the A56 there is an old hedge and ditch which runs into the garden and to the rear of Highfield Nursery Cottage Farm. Mr R Edwards (owner) said that the ditch within the garden had been piped and covered over by his father many years ago. The cottage itself stands close to what was the site of a much earlier inn, namely the Legs of Man. The old Chester road ran along the southeast side of this inn. The turnpike ran as the present A56.

113

SJ 4750/7320 Permission was given for an excavation in the garden between the old ditch and roadside hedge of the A56 which now fronts the cottage gardens. Removal of the top soil revealed sandstone chips which covered a layer of small stones intermingled with a blue/grey clay like material. The stoned surface went under the roadside hedge and maybe under the A56. The blue/grey clay material of 200mm had been laid upon a layer of pea grey gravels which was spread over the base red clay. (A construction similar to this was found on the Roman Holt road at Pulford near Chester). The excavation on the southeast side and closer to the old ditch revealed a surface of similar construction with larger pieces of sandstone in a row. Beyond this there was a later infill of clinker over the ditch pipe. A test trench was conducted on the far side of the ditch only to reveal a deep loamy soil and a base of natural red clay.

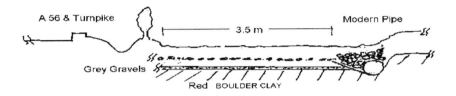

Highfield Nursery Cottage Farm, Dunham-on-the-Hill

WOOD FARM

A test trench was carried out in the A56 roadside field, southeast side SJ 4755/7360. In a gap of the modern hedge, the removal of top soil revealed sandstone chips and small pebble stones in a hard red material. There was no evidence of any gravels spread beneath. An old ditch line showed further away from the hedge, but between this and the hedge, a modern sewer pipe had been inserted destroying any further remains of what may have been the *Street*.

HORN'S MILL

From here the Roman route is suggested as the turnpike and the A56 to Horn's Mill Bridge by Helsby. Horn's Mill was originally a combined mill of water and wind power. It was reputed to have a date stone of 1775. There are no remains of the mill now except for the mill cottage. An under inspection of the bridge over the Horn's Mill brook revealed the remains of the old turnpike bridge alongside the modern A56 concrete bridge. The shallowness of the brook and the amount of shaped stones indicates the possibility of a ford. There was enough evidence found from aerial photographs to suggest the presence of an old road from the village of Ince to this ford. Beyond this another road branched and was traced through Alvanley, where it was known as the old 'Commonside Lane'.

HELSBY HILL

The hill is a rocky sandstone peninsula which stands above the Cheshire plains overlooking the old bay of the River Mersey. Iron Age tribesmen built a hill fort on the top of the hill and marked a northern frontier of their tribal territory. About 900AD a Norseman named Toki sailed from Ireland with his followers and family and settled in the Wirral. A frontier settlement was built at the base of the Helsby Hill, above the level of the undrained marsh land. They called it *'Hjallr-by'* (the village on the ledge). It was near the present Colliers' Square.

THE STREET

The turnpike from Horn's Mill continued as the A56 road through Helsby. The old Chester road leaves the turnpike just beyond the Three Ways Garage and is known as 'Robin Hood Lane'. The lane goes uphill and around the front of the hill and joins another lane known as 'The Sands.' This latter name indicates the continual falls of debris from the hill above. The 'Sands' turns sharply uphill and has been deeply cut through several large rocky outcrops, too high and too deep for any Roman road. It is doubtful whether the Romans would have a road that suffered from continual falling debris and would not have wanted to cut a road through these rock outcrops, when there is a much easier way.

ALTAR STONE

A Roman altar stone (held at Chester Museum) was found at SJ 4930/7560 in the Conery Field at the foot of a rocky outcrop to the front of the hill. (The old Chester road was cut through the rear of this outcrop). The outcrop is the first one uphill from the junction of Rake Lane. The field lay between the upper section of Rake Lane and the old Chester road. In the field there had been a spring. It was by this spring that the altar was found.

The field is now a fully developed estate. It is likely that the Roman road was on the same route as the old Chester road as far as the front of the hill to the meeting of Sands Lane and Rake Lane. Then the Roman route may have gone across Conery field where it would make a re-alignment on the stream of the spring. This alignment would take it through Colliers' Square. The square is in the vicinity of the original settlement.

(Roman roads normally only make re-alignments on fords or a brow of a hill).

From here an estimated line would take a possible route immediately across the front of Stocks Farm and onto the old Chester road. At Youd's Cottage the Chester road turned north, that now connects the old road to the A56 (turnpike road.)

The Altar Stone
The stone may have been a pillar stone, one commonly used as an indicator of a source of a fresh water supply or stream or a spring alongside a road. It displays on one side an axe and knife, and on the opposite side a 'patera' (jug) used for oblations on the altar.

YOUD'S COTTAGE
The cottage was built across the route of the old Chester road. From the rear of the cottage the road was traced northeast across Proffits Lane and into the present residential caravan site until it reaches another old ford at Irondish Brook. Roman coins and pottery (recorded by Chester Museum) have been found on the caravan site. Mrs Wright (owner) said that the front roadside garden was always wet and water would collect along the narrow path beside the front wall of the cottage. She allowed a two metre wide excavation in the front garden. The removal of 300mm of dark loamy soil, most of which had been imported over the years, revealed a layer of large cobbles.

These were set in a sticky wet brownish yellow sand and quite difficult to remove. The sand was troweled away to reveal a scatter of sandstone chips with small rounded pebbles rammed into a hard red material. A sectional trench was cut through this to reveal, 250mm below, a layer of blue/grey pea gravels of approximately 30mm, and this was laid on the natural red boulder clays. A test trench over the ditch on the southeast side revealed that it had been filled with rubble throughout its length causing a complete blockage for any water from the present road ditch.

Since the excavation in 1988 and a visit in 1994 to Youd's Cottage, Mrs Wright, has had all the large stones removed and the ditch piped, with a drain from the front garden. It is now free of standing water: she proudly shows that the Roman road forms a hard standing for a large fish tank. If anyone wishes to see the surface they would need to move the fish tank first! **See Map 3**

NETHERTON
SJ 5015/7610 Irondish Ford.
I enlisted the help of Mr W R Hawkin who specialised in the research of the Chester to Warrington turnpike. He said that the old Chester road had been made straighter and wider when the turnpike was constructed between Irondish and Netherton. The

116

village of Netherton is situated on the northwest side of the (turnpike) A56 prior to entering Frodsham. The old Chester road ran through the lower part of the village and then turned north. Beyond Dig Lane Farm and by the railway, the road returned northeast to enter Frodsham as the present main street.

HOWEY LANE SJ 5185/7730

Ivan Margary suspected that Howey Lane between Netherton and Overton village may have been the Roman road.

Overton village and its Saxon church is southeast of Netherton and on high ground just below the eastern side of Frodsham Hill.

During 1986 the Water Authority were cutting a trench across Howey Lane prior to the start of the incline. An inspection in this trench revealed several layers of tarmac, chippings, asphalt and sand, all laid onto bare sandstone rock. There was no evidence of any other road. In a garden on the southern side of Howey Lane an excavator was digging foundations for a new house. The driver obliged by cutting a deep trench from the lane hedge across the property of eight to ten metres displaying only bare rock beneath.

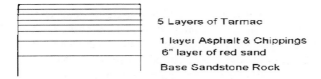

5 Layers of Tarmac

1 layer Asphalt & Chippings
6" layer of red sand

Base Sandstone Rock

Section of trench across Howey Lane cut by the Water Authority

SJ 5192/7741 In a field and on line of the lane and below the Church, a small test trench was cut across to find only sand on sandstone rock. The upper section of Howey Lane is very similar to the Sands Lane at Helsby where it has been cut deep through a high abutment of sandstone rock. This is too deep and too steep for any Roman road. Howey Lane was probably constructed in 1844 when councils had the power to enforce roads through private estates.

There is an even older road which runs between the rear of the Howey properties and close to the foot of Frodsham Hill. This went across the upper end of Howey Lane, indicating that Howey Lane was of a later date. Branching from this earlier road at the Dunsdale Gap, another track goes northwest, and it was the original termination of this that pinpointed the old Chester road.

117

SJ 5102/7700 Netherton. Here there had been a documented ford which, since the construction of the turnpike and improvements to minor roads, had been piped and built over.

Conclusion: It seems unreasonable to take a steeper and roundabout way to a River Weaver Ford when there is a much easier route.

OLD FRODSHAM

The land between Netherton and Frodsham must be imagined as it was, and not as it is today. There were two known water courses which crossed the old main street, though none are mentioned in any documentation about medieval Frodsham. It is also a known fact that previous to any improvement of existing roads these waterways would be open.

The stream that runs down from the Bellemont Vale (Overton Hill) to the old Frodsham shore line does not show the slightest trace of such a ford between Overton Hill and the railway, though evidence suggests that a ford may have been destroyed by the railway. If an estimated line was placed between the suspected ford and the old Chester road to Netherton, the line falls along the old Frodsham Castle Drive. This driveway was across the turnpike (A56) and terminated at the old Chester road on the north side of Netherton.

OLD CASTLE DRIVE

SJ 5125/7718. 1986. An excavation was made at the Netherton end of the castle drive between the eastern boundary of Dig Lane Farm and the A56. The top loamy soil of 250mm was removed to reveal a surface of small rounded pebbles rammed into a hard dark brown material of some 300mm depth. This was laid over a base surface of very hard red sand. The full width could not be determined because a small sand quarry had destroyed the east side of the track. To the west side, a row of larger stones was revealed and these may have formed a kerb. The ditch had been deepened, and a field pipe inserted and topped off with modern clinker.

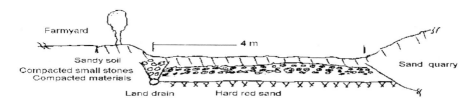

Old Castle Drive, Netherton

On modern maps the old drive is shown as a long wet hollow across the fields towards the castle entrance on the A56. On a visit in 1994 it was seen that the hollow track had been filled in and ploughed out. Only the trees that skirted the drive remain. **See Map 4**

FRODSHAM

Frodsham is situated on the southwest bank of the River Weaver. It emerges into history in Anglo-Saxon times as *Froda'sham*. This pre-conquest hamlet became the chief village of a large parish embracing Kingsley, Alvanley, Manley and Helsby, indicating a strong possibility that the church at Frodsham was a monastic missionary centre. The Domesday Book records that in 1066 the Manor of Frodsham belonged to the Saxon Earl Edwin of Mercia. The position of the borough on the old road from Chester to Warrington and the proximity of the rivers were important assets, and gradually a small but prosperous medieval market town developed. In the 18th century ship and boat building, and a salt refinery, were established here.

It would be very difficult to verify the route of a Roman road through the town because of the enlargement of the settlement since Anglo-Saxon times. Frodsham would not be any different from other towns which have sections of the main street on a Roman road, except where there have been modifications at a later period to the road system. High tides in 1720 did not reach above the cottages which line the west side of the main street and there is no evidence to suggest that the tides have ever come any higher.

CASTLE PARK.

TURNPIKE ROADS by G.N.Wright 1992. The Turnpike Act was mainly an improvement of an existing road. The local Turnpike Act of 1786 did not have the power to destroy or to enter private grounds for a thoroughfare. Its primary route around an estate boundary was paid for by a major local landlord at that time. Hence the reason why some turnpikes did not follow the original road. Here is another clue that the earlier road may have gone through the Frodsham Castle grounds.

The Roman road may have used part of Bridge Street and the remains of the turnpike immediately to the front of the Bridge Inn. At a later period, as at Handbridge in Chester, there would have been a wooden bridge over the river. *(Daniel Paterson 1811 in his book 'Roman Cheshire', page 352, mentions a wooden bridge over the Weaver at Frodsham).*

SUTTON WEAVER

Sutton Weaver lies northeast of Frodsham. Once a quiet rural village, it is now on the edge of a continual hum of moving traffic on the M56 motorway, the Runcorn freeway, the A56 and two busy railways. Amongst all this was a possible Roman road. The first clue is that of a Roman pavement (road surface) found on the northeast side of the River Weaver in 1888 at Marsh Gate Farm alongside the turnpike.

The question is whether it went to the Halton Fort before striking for Wilderspool or whether it went directly to Preston Brook. The second clue at SJ 5420/7950 lies in the fields north of the first bend of the A56 at Sutton Weaver. Here, there were remains of an old road, and judging its direction taken from the OS 1873 first edition map, it was going northwest to Halton.

THE HALTON ROAD

This old road continued the line of the turnpike (A56) from just beyond the present filling station above Marshgate Farm. A test trench was cut close to a field hedge. The only evidence that could be found was a scatter of small round pebbles intermingled with a yellow/orange clay. The fields had been ploughed before the hedge had been planted across the course of the track.

Where is the *Street* ?

The third clue was found by following the line of the old turnpike from the River Weaver northeast, past Marshgate Farm and the Filling Station. The turnpike then goes as the present A56. If the straight line is maintained, the old Chester road continues straight on as a hollow that runs to the top of the field. This hollow is slightly to the right of an electric pylon near the top of the field.

A fourth clue was found in the A56 road hedge across the top field. Here, there was a wide band of implanted holly SJ 5430/7935. This is where the old Chester road once passed through. The landowner said that this field had been ploughed quite regularly and he had noticed that in the hollow, the ground changed colour to a yellow/orange, and there was quite a wide band of stones to the top of the field.

The old road then went past the northwest side of a sixteenth century timber-framed building which stands to the rear (west side) of a thatched cottage alongside the turnpike (A56). The old road then falls onto the line of the turnpike at the front of Bank House Farm and just before the new bridge over the M56. It then continued alongside Park Farm by the Runcorn/Manchester railway. **See Map 5**

The only evidence in the field between Park Farm and the railway was an elongated hollow full of stagnant water with a stony bottom. The area beyond the railway was

120

all disturbed ground due to the Runcorn freeway and beyond that, a very large sports field which has been landscaped to the edge of Murdishaw Woods. The woods are on a shelf of dry ground above the Murdishaw Valley that runs northeast towards Preston Brook.

MURDISHAW WOODS
SJ 5600/8035 The next sighting of an old road was in the Murdishaw Woods that are along the northwest side of the M56. A raised feature of approximately ten metres wide was overplanted with trees. This can be traced until it disappears under the Whitehouse Industrial Busway. On the opposite side of the busway there was a hollow stony track which narrows and runs to an old ford on a crossing stream. On the far side of the stream the road runs for three metres and then becomes buried by infill of the motorway. An estimated line from the feature in the woods and the ford, goes under the M56 and through a new housing estate at Preston Brook. At the older village of Preston Brook there is a lane which has been blocked off from the new housing estate and the projected line falls along this lane. Had this been the old Chester road and Roman road?

PRESTON BROOK
On the east side of the A56 Canal Bridge there can be seen a hollow which may have been the *Street* to the brook. The line from the blocked lane falls along this hollow and onto the present lane which goes uphill to Preston-on-the-Hill. This lane is likely to be the continuation of a Roman road that had been found between Dunham Massey (Manchester) and Hatton Lane. *Margary's section of the Street branches from the canal bridge as the turnpike road (A56) for Warrington.* A short length of the turnpike road can be seen on the west side of the A56 as it leaves the canal bridge. **See Map 6**
THE END

Bewick Woodcut

CREDITS

It has taken almost eight years to find a suggested route for the *Street*. Every field has been walked, every track has been excavated within the vicinity of the turnpike. Many hours were spent at the record offices of Warrington and Chester. Several other roads came to light through all the field walking, and aerial photography revealed many unknown sites. These have all have been recorded with the appropriate Authorities. Thanks to Charles Harston for his help on excavations and putting up with my continued insistence; I am grateful to the farmers allowing the frequent walking of their land; Cheshire County Council Environmental Planning; Cheshire County Sites and Monuments Records Office, Chester; Warrington Records Office; British Rail Planning Dept; The River Weaver and Gowy Water Authority and the Grosvenor Museum. I thank also Edmund Waddelove (Ruthin) for his kind help and Frodsham & District Local History Group. The late W R Hawkin helped with the turnpike. Thank you to the householders of Helsby and Frodsham for allowing me into their gardens and a special word of thanks is extended to the local ladies who provided that refreshing cup of tea at the right time.

REFERENCE BOOKS

THE CHESTER TURNPIKE by W R Hawkin 1987
DISCOVERING CASTLE PARK by W R Hawkin & N Duncan 1989
ROMAN ROADS OF BRITAIN by I Margary London 1957
ROMAN CHESHIRE by D Paterson 1811
THE DUNHAM TRIANGLE by M S Wallace 1981
DISCOVERING OLD HELSBY by W R Hawkin 1991
ROMAN ROADS IN BRITAIN by T Codrington 1903
TURNPIKE ROADS by G N Wright 1992 (SHIRE PUBLICATIONS)

EX GRATIA

In the same series:-

HIDDEN
HIGHWAYS
OF
NORTH WALES

Ten Circular Walks exploring Roman Roads, Drovers' Ways, Packhorse Trails, Ancient Tracks, and Lost Lanes - and a Ghost Story

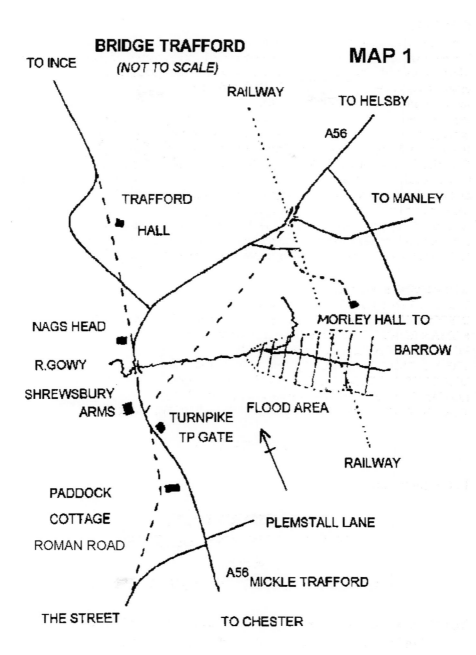

BRIDGE TRAFFORD
(NOT TO SCALE)

MAP 1

123

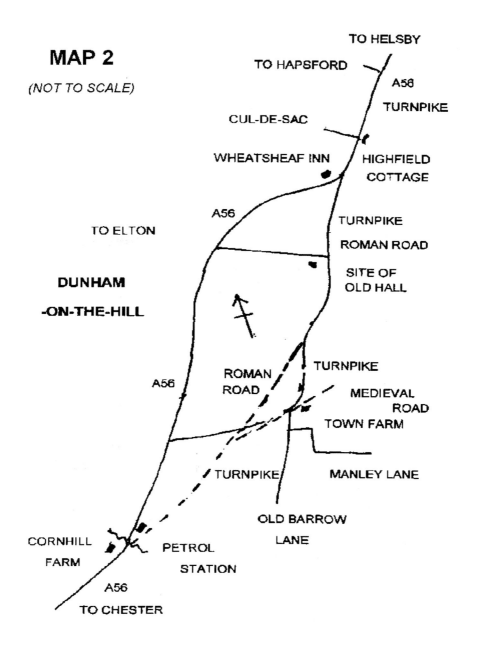

MAP 2

(NOT TO SCALE)

TO HELSBY

TO HAPSFORD

A56

TURNPIKE

CUL-DE-SAC

WHEATSHEAF INN

HIGHFIELD
COTTAGE

A56

TURNPIKE

TO ELTON

ROMAN ROAD

DUNHAM

SITE OF
OLD HALL

-ON-THE-HILL

ROMAN
ROAD

TURNPIKE

A56

MEDIEVAL
ROAD

TOWN FARM

MANLEY LANE

TURNPIKE

OLD BARROW
LANE

CORNHILL
FARM

PETROL
STATION

A56

TO CHESTER

124

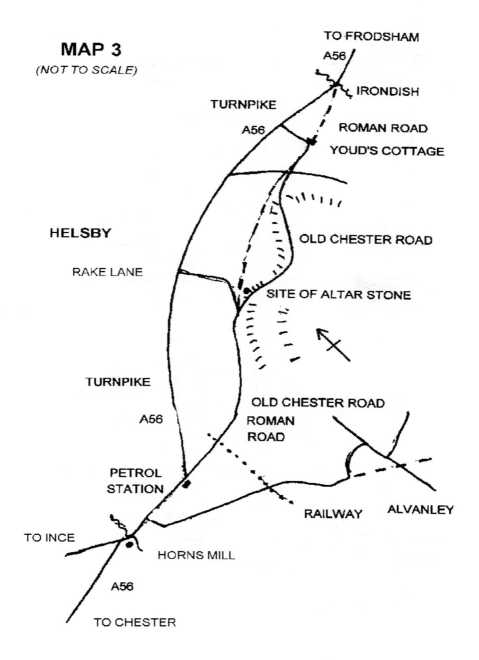

MAP 3
(NOT TO SCALE)

TO FRODSHAM

A56

IRONDISH

TURNPIKE

A56

ROMAN ROAD

YOUD'S COTTAGE

HELSBY

OLD CHESTER ROAD

RAKE LANE

SITE OF ALTAR STONE

TURNPIKE

OLD CHESTER ROAD

A56

ROMAN
ROAD

PETROL
STATION

RAILWAY

ALVANLEY

TO INCE

HORNS MILL

A56

TO CHESTER

125

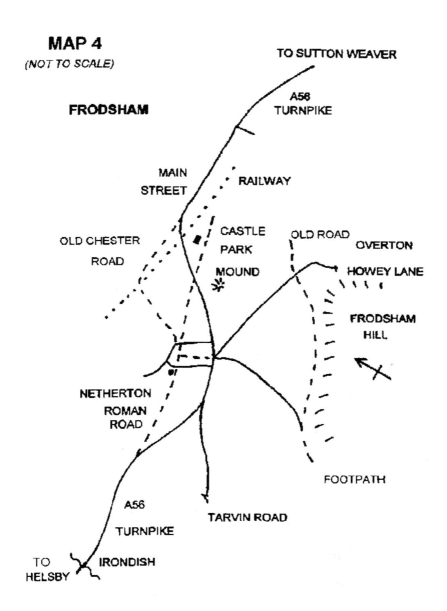

MAP 4
(NOT TO SCALE)

FRODSHAM

TO SUTTON WEAVER

A56
TURNPIKE

MAIN
STREET

RAILWAY

OLD CHESTER
ROAD

CASTLE
PARK

OLD ROAD

OVERTON

MOUND

HOWEY LANE

FRODSHAM
HILL

NETHERTON
ROMAN
ROAD

FOOTPATH

A56

TURNPIKE

TARVIN ROAD

TO
HELSBY

IRONDISH

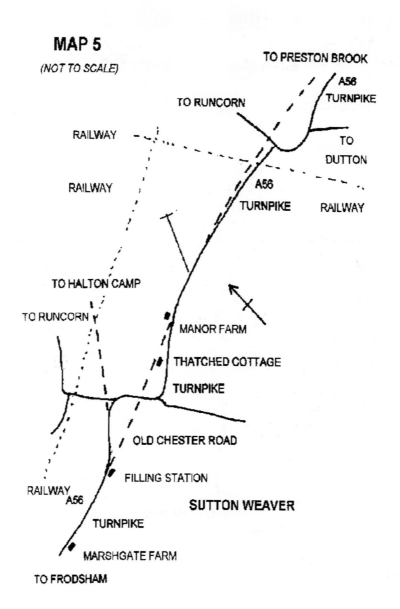

MAP 5
(NOT TO SCALE)

TO PRESTON BROOK

A56
TURNPIKE

TO RUNCORN

RAILWAY

TO
DUTTON

RAILWAY

A56
TURNPIKE

RAILWAY

TO HALTON CAMP

TO RUNCORN

MANOR FARM

THATCHED COTTAGE

TURNPIKE

OLD CHESTER ROAD

FILLING STATION

RAILWAY
A56

SUTTON WEAVER

TURNPIKE

MARSHGATE FARM

TO FRODSHAM

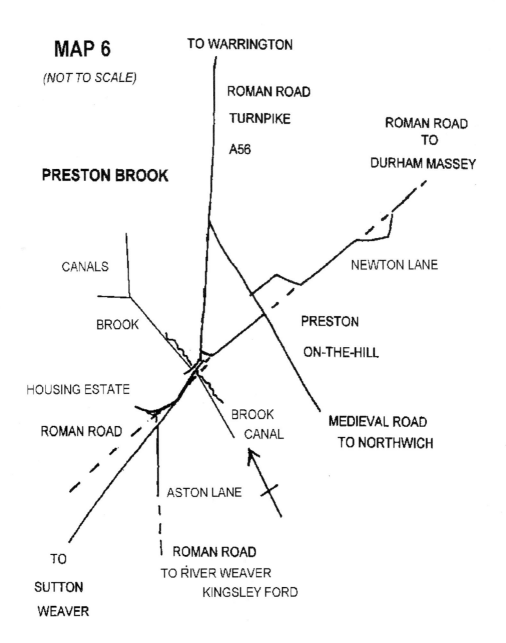

MAP 6

(NOT TO SCALE)

TO WARRINGTON

ROMAN ROAD

TURNPIKE

A56

ROMAN ROAD
TO
DURHAM MASSEY

PRESTON BROOK

CANALS

NEWTON LANE

BROOK

PRESTON

ON-THE-HILL

HOUSING ESTATE

ROMAN ROAD

BROOK

CANAL

MEDIEVAL ROAD
TO NORTHWICH

ASTON LANE

TO

SUTTON

WEAVER

ROMAN ROAD
TO RIVER WEAVER
KINGSLEY FORD